THE
BOOK
I DIDN'T
WANT
TO
WRITE

THE
BOOK
I DIDN'T
WANT
TO
WRITE

ERWAN LARHER

Translated from the French by **Brent Keever**

LOCARNO PRESS

· VANCOUVER ·

Published in 2018 by Locarno Press
locarnopress.com

First published in France under the title
Le Livre que je ne voulais pas écrire © Quidam Éditeur 2017

Text © Erwan Larher 2017
English translation © Brent Keever 2018

CIP data is available from Library and Archives Canada
ISBN 978-1-988996-00-4

Printed in Canada
10 9 8 7 6 5 4 3 2 1

Cover design by Paul Hodgson
Typeset by Elisa Gutiérrez
Edited by Scott Steedman

"As Seen from Outside" passages written by Jérôme Attal, Charlotte Becquin, Frédéric Burel, Manuel Candré, Jeanne Doe, Manon Fargetton, Bertrand Guillot, Paul Larher, Philippe Larher, Églantine Le Coz, Delphine Nahon, Loulou Robert, Sigolène Vinson, and Alice Zeniter.

1

YOU LISTENED TO ROCK. Rock razor-wired with guitars and anger. You've been listening to it since before you were a teen. As a kid, you needed your parents' permission to use the stereo. An endless enchantment. How you loved pushing that little lever to get the arm to lift off, the arm that held the needle at its end, a needle you would place above the edge of the record while closing one eye for more precision. The platter would start to turn. Then you would let it drop, always with the help of the little lever. It was all about not missing your shot; then the diamond stylus hit the LP with a crackle. In a few seconds the living room throbbed with a magical energy, that wrapped around you as if the music had always been inside you and those big speakers your father had made just had to bring it to life.

The Leonard Cohen cassette, the Beatles' red and the blue double albums, the Cologne Concert that was a little worn around the edges. These were sacred objects.

At the same time, you were bewitched by the voodoo of words, of books devoured, everywhere, all the time, famished. But with music, the spell was more immediate and spontaneous. More *natural?* Physical. It took over, moved in, without you having to learn how, without fingers that would follow the lines, without brows furrowed by intricate syllables. You sang Brassens and Brel. You wailed out the Grand Orchestre du Splendid, Eddy Mitchell, and Renaud during road trips, even if the lyrics didn't always make sense.

You were barely a teenager when FM stations hit the airwaves. Everything was suddenly right at your fingertips. You could record—by pushing *play* and *record* at the same time—Alain Bashung and Depeche Mode, the Police and Kim Wilde, the Stray Cats, and unknown groups on local radio stations.

"That's punk."

David Imbert's verdict was indisputable. You were twelve, and he was fourteen. Your middle school class was on a fieldtrip near Chamonix. You had just had David listen to your favorite song from your latest music mix, recorded on a 90-minute BASF Chrome cassette. The 120-minute cassettes were too fragile, and the tape often got tangled; the 60-minute cassettes were too short to get an album on one side, so one of them would make you miss out on the end of a Sex Pistols song for a long time, so you would be stunned years later to hear the whole song, because you were so used to it being cut off in the middle of a chorus.

You usually wrote down the name of the song and the group on the cassette's liner notes, but sometimes the radio presenter didn't tell you. Other times you would jot down what you heard—"Original Sin" by In Nick Says, a group whose records you could never found in the supermarket where you followed your mother, in the hope that she would give in to your begging. "Come on, Mom, pleeeeease, just one single …"

For David, happy to be called a "badass" by your friends—you never dared ask what that adjective meant—INXS is crap. Over his leather jacket, he wore a sleeveless denim vest embroidered with badges. Each one invoked an equally powerful and disturbing universe: a zeppelin on fire, a cannon on wheels, a skeleton in a wedding dress … We called him Donald because he imitated Donald Duck so well. You remember his nickname while writing down this scene. The amount of information that unknowingly sleeps in you is frightening. You can also clearly recall that steep path in the middle of the forest where you questioned David, after having him listen to an unknown song that put you into a trance on your Walkman, hoping that he would know the artist.

"It's punk. So, you like punk."

"What's punk?"

The Internet was just a mad scientist's dream. You were reading detective and adventure novels. You grew up in Ballans, in the Charentes-Maritime region, a village with 282 inhabitants lost in the middle of Pineau vineyards. You had only kissed one girl, and only once, without slipping her the tongue.

"Well, punk … Punk is … Listen, give me a blank cassette. I'll record some stuff for you."

You accepted. David put together an A-side of Téléphone (*Au Coeur de la nuit*) and a B-side of AC/DC for you.

You owed your first real encounter with punk to Yann Mahé, at the Moëlan-sur-Mer middle school in grade ten. Yann was almost fifteen, you were barely thirteen. He wore tight tartan pants and army boots and had a few whiskers over his upper lip and on his chin. Your face was hairless. He was at war with his father, superintendent of the school. It had never crossed your mind to upset your own father, much less talk back to him. Yann's family lived in staff housing virtually on the schoolyard. Would that even be possible today? Over lunch hour, he would sometimes have you over to listen to music. You were dumbfounded to discover that you could sing "I fuck my dad, I fuck my mom, I fuck my grandmother up the ass," get it recorded on an album, and that that album could be perfectly legally sold on the racks. You discovered the Sex Pistols, Chaos en France, the Exploited, UK Subs, Métal Urbain, Bérurier Noir, and other belching, pulsing thrills. At Melody, the record shop at Quimperlé, you could easily listen to punk rock records all afternoon long if you wanted. You would buy the albums of Oberkampf, Special Duties, Virgin Prunes, the Stranglers, later the first six Noir Désir singles, and many others. Almost all your pocket money would go there.

You listened to rock, the soundtrack of your tormented soul. You were that music, utterly. It defined you. Adults and most of your peers—people who saw music as just entertainment, a background, a decorative sonic accessory—didn't understand this. "He'll get over it," they would say.

Rock—gateway to invisible worlds, revelation of the whorls of your soul, and catalyst of your imagination, just like words. At fourteen, while at boarding school, you started to write your first "novel" (always in quotes), where a privileged place was given to the tortured, melancholic songs—sometimes bright, although lit by a black light—of certain artists of the time. The Cure, in particular. You were convinced that Robert Smith was your cosmic twin.

You listened to rock, so you were part of a family. We could recognize each other with a glance. We would have excited discussions about records, influences, and styles. We would exchange bootleg tapes, and go to more or less permitted concerts. In Brittany, you would see almost the entire French alternative scene parading through bars, night clubs, or simple barns. With the Wampas, French Lovers, Les Satellites, Washington Dead Cats, Jad Wio, or Dominic Sonic.

You listened to rock. Music was at the center of everything, with poetry. You worshipped Mallarmé. During your last year in school, you wrote songs for Charlotte Corday, a group for which you were the "singer" (always in quotes). Then, with your exploding hairdo and black mascara under your eyes, you got to Versailles to do your pre-college prep courses. Yann would miss out on your new wave infidelities. He would not see the '90s. Suicide. The last time you saw him, during a pirate rock concert, he tried to get a little cash out of you. Over those seven or eight years of strange, spaced-out friendship, you saw and understood nothing. Gullible, you did not know what that word people would whisper about him implied—*junkie*.

Then there was the Velvet Underground, MC5, the Stooges, the Sonics. When grunge and fusion hit, you were ready.

Rock. An outlet for that well-mannered, obedient child you were, who would not transgress for a million dollars, who missed out on his adolescent crisis, who spent two years in a military school. You never had a fit of anger—Joe Strummer had them for you. You followed the rules, you never made waves, you were never bold enough to dye your hair red or have a Mohawk, but you listened to rock. Whose raging energy both jived with and fed the anger that slept in you, the anger those efforts to look like the model son everybody wanted you to be had smothered.

Was it a coincidence that David Imbert found out you liked punk at the very moment you were faced for the first time with the violence of the world, without being prepared for it? From elementary to middle school, you grew up in the Charente countryside, surrounded by children, grandchildren, and great-grandchildren of Charente parentage. We knew each other, talked to each other, hated each other, ran into each other, avoided each other, had each other over, helped each other out. We set money aside to buy the grape-harvesting machine, borrowed a tractor or a flatbed, swapped rabbits for chickens, clashed and came together over a trifle. Sometimes at church. At ten, in the middle of the school year, you ended up in a suburban middle school that drew in the descendants of Algerian Jewish, Italian, Spanish, and North African immigrants, as well as a few gypsies. That is what we called them, "gypsies." You did not know what that meant, except for the image of a woman on your parents' cigarette packs. You were made to learn that the male model was not to be trusted. There were gangs, groups, and underlying tensions that would explode in quick, sudden fights. You had to avoid the snitches, and the headmaster was no softy. This violence shot through you, an awkward kid who had not yet entered adolescence. You were afraid at each recess, afraid in the hallways, afraid in the cafeteria, afraid in the bus. With a fear that you did not show or express, certainly not in front of your parents. You were already very proud.

In this middle school, you had the first and, up to now, last fight of your life. David Tournadre called you a son of a bitch. God only knows what got into you. You answered back, "I'll be waiting for you after school." He answered "All right" before you had the time to take it back. Serious disagreements were settled like this at that time at school—with a fight outdoors, on a kind of bare lawn planted with chestnut trees to the right of the entrance. You were one year older, though you looked young for your age. You did not have a very assertive personality. If you think about it, you must have unwittingly decided on that day to go through an initiation rite by standing up to one of the bullies of your class. You were stressed out all day long. You were wearing a white Saint-James pullover that was itchy, but you liked it a lot. You took it off—no way were you going to damage or dirty it. There was one rule: no low blows. You do not have a very clear memory of the fight, except that it was short (the school buses did not wait for scores to be settled), and there was no real victor. A black eye for him and a split lip for me.

Was it the idylls of your childhood years that created your revulsion to all forms of violence? At seven or eight, you started practicing judo. You did not like to go to practice, you were scared to get hurt, you hated fights, so you switched to soccer. You had daredevil pals. You were careful. Or to put it another way, cowardly. You did a little skateboarding, you were always afraid of falling down, and you gave it up. When others would climb high up trees, you would stop at the lowest branches. On top of that, you had vertigo. You were never an adventurer: you would rather set out for the high seas with Long John Silver on your couch. Your whole life, you have avoided punches, fights, and scuffles, even tackles during your American football years. As a miracle, or because you never went looking for them. You separated brawlers, calmed down situations, appeased tensions. Not the kind to throw oil on the fire. It might have been your height that helped you avoid trouble with fighters without even knowing it. Though you did hang out in sketchy bars, grungy nightclubs, sports arenas, and some fairly seamy concerts, sometimes in the weirdest places. The only blow you almost took since your schoolyear scuffle came from a woman you were breaking up with. She weighed fifty pounds less than you and was ten inches shorter. You finagled your way out of it. As you did another night when you were twenty-four and the telephone rang in your room in Pigalle. A worked-up guy with a "riffraff" accent, as we said at the time, promised you that he was going to find you and "cut off your balls." Your girlfriend was his ex, she had left him and he wanted her back. She had told you that he was a little bit of a gang leader, a bit of a dealer, and a lot dangerous. You spent half an hour on the phone with him. At the end of the conversation, he was crying. No more talk of attacking your genital zone. You even offered to go get a drink together. You were relieved that he refused.

Does your obsessive fear of violence spring from your wimpiness? You almost fainted in science class while watching a film on bone marrow transplants. You almost blacked out while having your pelvis X-rayed. You almost fainted at the theater while watching a Quentin Tarantino film. You swoon over the simplest bloodwork or shot. And when it comes to dentists …

Kindhearted souls say that you are overly sensitive. Wisecrackers prefer "sissy." That could be surprising given how little your body type corresponds to these weaknesses. People think you are bold, brash, and forthcoming when you are, at best, wary. You hope you are being neither wussy nor craven. To your credit, you have remained faithful to punk rock, unlike some of your acquaintances who have aged into jazz, or worse, world music. The attire of adulthood has never been a suit of armor against violence, no more than the fear of death has.

Violence? It is coming.

As Seen from Outside: I

10 AM, NOVEMBER 14

The neighborhood is deserted. A gathering on rue Bichat, in front of Le Petit Cambodge and Le Carillon. I am not going. We will go there tomorrow as a family. Max will lay down a flower among many others. Mausoleum, symbols that will remain there for weeks before their gradual, modest withdrawal.

The sky is clear. Very sunny, but I am cold. Angry too. The feeling of being at the heart of a freezing, morbid reality.

Another feeling. This one undefinable, like the desire, the need to hold and protect the people that I run into this morning. It is them, neighbors and friends, who took the bullets that night. This is my neighborhood. This is me.

5 AM

It will be hard for me to fall asleep. But at least I know now. He is alive.

I've just had J. on the phone. He took a bullet in the butt. We will laugh about it, and he will suffer through it. A Sunday hospital visit confirms this. Stretched out on his bed, cocky and funny as usual, but livid. Don't know if it's only from the physical pain. All three old buddies reunited, we don't question it. Modesty and relief. Being with him, sharing red wine and dried sausages, is enough for us.

3 AM

This night is endless and nameless.

Johanna and I walk across the Place de la
République and go up the rue Grange-aux-Belles. The
few police who are still there are blocking access by
the rue Faubourg du Temple and Bichat. We don't
question them about it, obviously.

He is still not answering the phone. The wait is far
too long. Where is that man who they were calling
"the friend of the Bataclan" on social media? And still
so many questions: Why wasn't I with him? Was he
at least helped? We should have been together that
evening at the concert, and I could have ... Could have
what? Protected him? Drawn him away from this
horror through the sheer effect of my presence? What
nonsense! This guilt, which has no place in front of the
pain of others, will only go away for a while.

Midnight

Near République and the Bataclan, at C. and J.'s place.
A birthday party, rather than going to a concert with
buddies.

Already sickening TV images, worried, disoriented
faces, alcohol that I gulp down in big, tranquilizing
swigs. Down on the street there are crowds in
incomprehensible motion, out of sync with the
televised reality. And for two hours now, those sirens,

coming from everywhere, of all kinds, that will make up the morbid soundtrack of this night.

He is not answering his phone. Panic attacks. But not just that. There's another feeling, indescribable, like something unthinkable. The impossible cannot happen. He is strong, sly, lucky. He always gets by.

At our place, on the other side of the Canal, the children are not alone. The cousins have joined them. They ask us questions over the phone. I have no answers, just words meant to reassure.

9 PM, NOVEMBER 13

Nina is 17. Discussions with her, when she is open to them, are always bubbly.

Massive Attack are on the radio. Music sometimes has the ability to evoke a moment, a period. I explain this to Nina: Massive Attack are 1998. A lucky year: her birth, France winning the World Cup, a credible left-wing in power. It's a carefree year. 2001, and the Twin Towers, will be in three years.

As Johanna is getting ready, one last question for the children before we leave. I will order them a meal, and they will go pick it up: Pizzeria or Le Petit Cambodge? Pizza it is, which is closer. Their laziness makes me smile. I must have been the same.

It's 9:25 pm. From our scooter, we see the owner of Le Petit Cambodge running on the sidewalk. He must be late to work. We turn on rue Bichat. The cross section is blocked. A police officer cordons off the street. An accident? I turn around, and a young girl, a pink helmet on a scooter, goes up the street and passes in front of us, screaming. It's a hot time in the neighborhood tonight.

2

O N NOVEMBER 26, early evening, you were at the Trabendo with Fred and Guillaume. With beers in hand, you were chatting merrily while waiting for the start of the Blood Red Shoes concert. A slightly dirty boogie rock coming from the speakers suddenly drew your attention. Love at first beat. You asked Guillaume, a riff specialist who smells of axle grease and sweat, about it. He didn't know them. You wanted to know. You had to know. Had to gather the information before the song ended. You rushed to its source, a sound engineer behind his mixer. He answered "Eagles of Death Metal," without even raising his eyes. You thought about a joke, but you weren't familiar enough with the Sussex accent.

So you can't even brag about having discovered EODM before everybody else (you can gladly show off about Offspring, however, but that's a long story), or about having listened to them since their beginning (unlike Noir Désir or the White Stripes), because, as the Internet taught you once you got back home, they had released their first album four years earlier, in 2004.

On August 30, 2009, EODM were on the lineup for Rock en Seine. For a good week, Poopy would listen to them in the car, in the apartment, and spilling out of your headphones. You didn't like all of their tracks, so be it, but you loved the ones you did. So Poopy, your future wife (or at least, so you thought at the time; you cancelled the wedding five months later, two months before the final payments were due; she has remained your best friend) gives you a ticket to the music festival for your birthday. In the late afternoon, under a blazing sun, you got forty-five minutes of murky, sour sound—a plate of chewy magma that had all gone to pot. You quickly forgot that disappointment because the thing you would remember from that day was Fred's face when you asked him right after the concert if he would like to be your best man. And his modest and kind "Yeah."

September 14, 2015, at 5:18 pm, you got an e-mail from the ticket website summarizing your order: "1 ticket, Regular Price only, for EAGLES OF DEATH METAL (LE BATACLAN, PARIS 11), Friday 11/13/2015 at 7:30 pm. Total 30.70 EUR." With the service taking €0.50 ("processing fees"), you paid €31.20. Without a moment's hesitation. As soon as the information reached you saying that EODM were giving this concert in Paris, you got online to buy your ticket.

September 14, 2015, at 5:21 pm, you sent an e-mail to Guillaume, Fred (the best man at the non-wedding), and Florian to tell them about your purchase and push them to imitate you. November 13, 2015, at 9:29 am, using the "Custom Privacy" option on Facebook that blocks the field of vision of those "Unknown" members of your list (about 75% of your virtual friends), you sent the following message:

Erwan Larher
13 novembre 2015 · ✿ ▼

Ce soir au Bataclan, on boit de la mauvaise bière, on saute sur place en braillant "I really wanna be in L.A.", gloire au mauvais goût et au bon rock, j'aurai mes santiags aux pieds.

Eagles of Death Metal - I Want You So Hard

Music video by Eagles of Death Metal performing I Want You So Hard. (C) 2008 Downtown Records

YOUTUBE.COM

👍 J'aime   💬 Commenter   ↗ Partager

🔵 Raphael Anciaux, Marie Dô et 26 autres personnes

Erwan Larher
November 13, 2015 ✿ ▼

Tonight at the Bataclan, we are going to drink bad beer and jump up and down while howling "I really wanna be in L.A." All hail bad taste and good rock. I'll be wearing my cowboy boots.

Eagles of Death Metal - I Want You So Hard

Music video by Eagles of Death Metal performing I Want You So Hard. (C) 2008 Downtown Records

YOUTUBE.COM

👍 Like   💬 Comment   ↗ Share

🔵 Raphael Ancaux, Marie Dô, and 26 other people like this.

You got an answer from your friend Yves, a grand buccaneer of rock concerts in the eyes of the Lord:

Yves Garrot Je n'en suis pas, hélas, restriction budgétaire oblige.....
J'aime · Répondre · 13 novembre 2015, 13:50

Erwan Larher Oh... J'étais presque certain de t'y croiser, (faux-) cousin... Déception.

Yves Garrot Alas, I can't make it. Budgetary restrictions say no.
Like • Reply • November 13, 2015, 13:50

Erwan Larher Oh, I was almost sure to run into you there, (false) friend. Let down.

November 13, 2015, around 8:15 pm (please note how we are almost finished with precise facts), you parked your Honda Shadow right across from the Bataclan, on the strip at the intersection of Richard Lenoir and Voltaire boulevards. You walked across the strip. Few people in front of the concert hall. You got there well after the doors opened, not keen on listening to the opening act. You were alone. Your friends could not come. Jeanne preferred working on her kicks and punches at French boxing practice. You would find out later that, individually (because they didn't know each other), two friends had been thinking about surprising you there.

You took the time to smoke a cigarette, then you went into the lobby.

Pause. Rewind. You crossed the boulevard—did you turn your head to the left? See anything? Play. Pause. You finished your smoke on the sidewalk—did you look at the cars parked in front of the concert hall? In front of the Bataclan Café? You have crossed that boulevard a thousand times, smoked the same butt a thousand times, in slow motion, drilling into your memory, scraping up images worn away by a lack of attention. Was their car already there? With a sharp sense of orientation and a good photographic memory, could you have sighted them? Were they in your field of vision at a certain time? Soon only rough-hewn impressions will remain of this cigarette and that crossing. The scene becomes false and faked because you have played it over too often in your head. Nothing sensational ever comes from it. You saw nothing out of the ordinary. You sensed no dark omen. You strolled across Voltaire with your cig in your mouth, took the last puffs in front of the hall—nothing dramatic—then showed your ticket to the bouncers and went in.

You went up the steps, dropped your coat and your helmet off at the check-stand. You can still today see a bit of scotch tape on your helmet that held the numbered ticket stub, whose other half was given to you by a pretty young woman with a smile. You refuse to remove it.

You put the stub in your jeans, in the back pocket. The only skinny jeans in your wardrobe. You thought they looked good on you. You had bought them a few months earlier, whereas for years you had sworn that you would never slide into a pair of skinnies. Let's hope that you can be faithful to baggy-fit … Your front pockets hold your pack of cigarettes, a lighter, and thirty euros.

You went into the concert hall. Familiar sensations. Immediate bliss. A rock concert. You can't count them anymore, but every time it's the same magic, the same thrill. Come on, go ahead, you can now say that if you had to have one regret in life, it would be to have not become a rock star.

You smiled.

From then on, it was no longer your story. Not *only* your story.

From then on, it was no longer only your story. It was also our story.

From then on, war, chaos, big, sensationalist, scaremongering headlines. We want to know everything. Tell us the story. Don't leave out any details.

From then on, political exploitation. Stiff chins, stern faces in front of the camera, hawkish declarations. You'll see what we're going to do. Choose your side. *Aux armes, citoyens!* Johnny, get your gun.

From then on, generation this and generation that, openly international philosophers became French, others found their faith, or their voice, again. "I told you so." We found our places to park, minds in double-parking mode, without our warning lights.

From then on, a before, and an after.

From then on, I leave things out, I falsify, I may be lying. First names no longer have anything personal about them. You are going to have to get used to it.

From then on, a story that I didn't want to tell begins.

3

"BUT YOU HAVE TO TELL IT!"

Manuel was vehement. Seated across from you in the high-speed train taking you from Annecy to Paris, he was giving you a piece of his mind. Alice, next to him, seemed to have taken his side. It was surreal. A few minutes earlier, you had been laughing like brats, shooting out jokes and more-or-less-successful puns. The banter must have hit a blank spot, or one adjective altered its playful path. In a second, Manuel can go from joyful to sullen. On top of being bearded, funny, and a novelist, he has broad shoulders and impressive pecs that he can flex one at a time. But you had never seen him furious at you. He is usually as sweet as a peach. Your arguments for refusing to recount your experiences at the Bataclan five months earlier did not convince him now. In sum, you had argued that you believed in a thoughtful press able to explain the upheavals of this world to the public, the opposite of the reigning human-interest press (which provokes inhuman disinterest, as Pierre Bourdieu might have said). You didn't want to offer your tearful contribution to that emotional ocean on which the media of the society of spectacle loves to surf.

"You can't lump all journalists together," Manuel cautioned, with his booming, angry, Papa Bear voice.

The heads of your nearest fellow travelers turned toward your trio, then plunged back into their entertainment—a sandwich, a film, a magazine, a video game. You didn't think that you had lumped anyone together. You just didn't want to testify, that's all. You had turned down dozens of offers already, from all over the world, some even the day after it happened. Some scribblers spared nothing, and certainly not moralizing, to try to convince you. "Think about your books. Five pages in our paper would be good for your sales!"

"He's right, isn't he?"

Of course he was right. You had published four novels, whose total sales over six years have brought in barely the equivalent of six months' salary at minimum wage. You knew what kind of media, hence financial, profit your novels could make from your status as a Bataclan survivor. It would have been so easy to say yes. To betray yourself.

"Stop!" Papa Bear roared. "You're getting on my nerves with your 'Mr. Above-It-All' attitude. If you were such a saint you wouldn't flaunt your refusal to tell your story like an act of bravery. You wouldn't even talk about it."

You weren't a saint. You were trying to balance your values with your actions. It wasn't always easy. A (small) part of you felt (a little bit) badly about the inflexibility of the other. Getting congratulated for that inflexibility did your ego good, comforted you in where you stood. No reason to roar or snarl, or even less to jabber. What's more, had we questioned the sensationalist spew of those

"Bataclan Seen From the Inside" stories? Do you have to talk under the pretext that there's a microphone dangling there? To exhibit yourself because the camera is rolling? You always have to justify refusing, never accepting. Do those who bribe the nonstop news channels with their race for the scoop abstain from reading the testimony of survivors?

"But you don't understand that we need that," Alice jabbed at you. "What happened that night touched, devastated, and shocked all of us."

"Of course we pounced on the slightest bit of news."

"To know, to understand, and to get over the shock," butted in a guy sitting not far away dressed in Austrian wool.

"Broadcast on a loop, all night long and over the following days," added a wrinkly old woman. "I even read *Libé*."

What was I getting myself into? Those passengers getting into my brain, from a virtually empty train car, were taking Alice and Manuel's side, ganging up against you. You waffled. Contrary to appearances, you had never been very sure of yourself. Fickle? Not, not to that point. Gullible? That's debatable. As soon as it comes to asserting your opinions, even when it comes to clothing, you lose your resources. Underneath your self-assured and swashbuckling airs, you have neither the sense of repartee nor good timing. Writing novels helps you skirt these shortcomings.

"You can't condemn people who testify," Alice retorted.

"Talking might be a way to heal for them."

"You can be healed through talking, of course. A host of therapies exist. But why talk in public?" you objected. "Are we required to put our lives and desires on display, to spread out our personal goods, our tiniest opinions? We are caught up in an endless flood of sounds, signs, and icons. Tubes, screens, and radio waves spew relentlessly. We can't analyze anymore. Don't have the time for it. Those who can do so are drowned out by news, events, the immediate. In raw emotion. In the sensational."

Manuel burst out laughing.

"Blah, blah, blah, blah, blah! When are you going to stop making excuses for yourself, huh?"

Good Lord! That night, you didn't do anything that deserves to be known about, recognized, pondered upon, transmitted, commented on by your peers! You didn't do anything that could serve as an example. You lay down on the floor, you took a point-blank bullet, and you were getting by without too much trouble. What's the link with your work as a novelist and your books? You've hoped that they'd be read for the right reasons, chosen for a love of literature. Don't you have the right to reflect on the consequences of your actions before accepting an interview for *Paris Match* or *Télérama?*

"*Match* and *Télérama* are the not the same thing, not the same thing as BFM TV!"

Oh yes they are, Manuel. In the weeks following the attacks of November 13, 2015, it was the same thing. The same indecency oozed out of the messages of every journalist, on your cell phone, in your e-mail box, on Facebook. You had refused to tell your story. You decreed that you would write nothing about the Bataclan—at least not immediately, not in the frenzy, in the immediacy, without taking a step back. The passengers started protesting soon enough. You closed your eyes. They still don't exist.

"Are you okay?" Alice worried?

Nothing would ever be normal again. You knew from then on that the absurd could occur everywhere, and at any moment. You opened your eyes in the peace of car number 17.

"You have to tell it," Manuel hammered on. "If you can't do it for yourself, do it for the others. You are a writer. Because of that, how you relate this event interests us."

He started to argue as if your brain were just as developed as his. Your writing had to embody the page, the content the vessel. Subvert rather than criticize the medium, embodying a fiction without narrative. What is a language but the primacy of a precision within the movement from whence it springs? You told him that you might be getting hungry. Your friend has an appetite to go with his frame. The idea of skipping a meal is blasphemy to him. You wondered how he would have stood the restricted diet of your first days in hospital.

You bleated out that if nobody wanted to know how the events occurred, there would be no need to tell the tale. "Minute-by-minute" reconstitutions had been published here, there, and everywhere.

"That's exactly because those people told the story of how it occurred."

If you accepted, you argued, they would ask your opinion. But you don't have an opinion; well, in fact you do, but a changing, citizen's opinion that tries to reflect calmly. An opinion speckled with question marks, the opposite of those decisive, definitive opinions that generates *likes* and *views*. You are neither a sociologist, nor a philosopher, nor a thinker. Being a victim grants you no authority to give your shaky, see-through opinion on the television or in a weekly paper. Not all words have worth.

"We don't give a damn about your opinion. We want an epic!" Manuel replies.

Manuel and Alice had you in a good-cop/bad-cop stranglehold, sharpening the fangs of their respective acumen. Yours still has its baby teeth. They were demolishing the corners they had pushed you in.

"You have to share it."

You squinted while staring at Alice. You could either sit back in your seat and nod, or stay there with your mouth agape. Did you answer? Say something like, "Yes, that's an argument, the only worthy one"?

At any rate, something clicked in you. Because Alice pronounced the magic word "share"? It's not even certain that it passed through her lips. But even if everything is fictionalized, both of your well-meaning friends who were ganging up on you were right. Despite yourself, you had been granted a kind of mission. It was not the testimony of Erwan Larher that mattered. What mattered was what the only writer present on that night at the Bataclan would produce if they set to work on the subject, the matter at hand.

The only writer. Lucky you.

"Erwan, a book! Erwan, a book!" the passengers in the empty car bellowed, those characters of your dilemma, the multiple copies of yourself.

Manuel got up and put on his jacket.

"I am going to the bar," he said. "This isn't over, but this story has made me hungry."

As Seen from Outside: II

I loathe all modern, impersonal means of communication. I can't get over speaking in front of a screen, and even less over the telephone. However, there are so many questions I would have liked to ask you after what you experienced last November. But it's only face-to-face that I would have wanted to do it ... In a way, I am a little jealous of all the people who were with you in the hours, in the days that followed. Jealous of all your wonderful friends who were really there for you, and for us, so far away, by keeping us informed in an almost live feed. I would have also liked to have been next to you, to talk to you, or to say nothing. But to be there. To share with you, in one way or another, and maybe to help you. But how do you know the right thing to say, the right thing to do? That ease in doing things naturally, going with your feelings, is foreign to me. Today, you are giving me, giving us, a chance to express ourselves and to get back to those, for me, unimaginable hours. I should make the most of this to ask you those questions that crossed my mind at one time or another last November. But isn't it selfish and cruel to force you to return to those surely horrible moments that you might not want to bring up? Isn't this misplaced curiosity and voyeurism? Is it a taboo to talk about death, pain, fear, and powerlessness? What's more, were you scared during those long moments spent on the floor in the Bataclan concert hall? Scared of what? Scared of whom? Did you think about death even once? Your own? That of the people around you? Do we think about other people at such times? Are ties created with your partners in misfortune? Do we look at each other? Speak to each other? Do we feel pain? Does it take the upper hand over everything else? It's funny how my questions have gone from "you" to "we" ... It seems that these are really difficult topics to address directly. We ... You ... I don't know how to go on. Were you only thinking about the present moment? Were you making plans, making projects, making resolutions? Something like, "If I get out of this alive, I will ..." Did you keep your eyes open? Did you want to close them? Did you regret some moments in your life, some choices, some acts? Do you still regret them today? Did you cry? Was there pain? Sadness? Did you learn something about yourself? What? Are you different now? How? Was this the most important event in your life, something that will mark you forever? Are you angry with someone? And then all those questions forgotten over time. And do you want to ask me, ask us some questions?

4

A FEW DAYS AFTER YOUR RAILWAY CONVERSATION with Manuel and Alice, you were woken up at the crack of dawn by sentences squawking in your skull. That happens to you sometimes. You took the notebook and pen from your nightstand. And so the book, this book, began to be written. Without you. Ever since, you'd been running after it. To master and tame it. And it endlessly eluded you.

It eluded you because the act of writing came before the decision to write. For weeks, you were torn between the stubbornness of words and your will to not turn your misfortune into a text, a will that gave in when something obvious doused you. You were stuck at the crossroads of an individual ordeal and a collective shock, on the pivot point between "I" and "We."

Since the first spray of steel, all has been a question about your own survival, about getting through it. About overcoming your fears—what after-effects?—and your pain. A personal, private tragedy. Like every personal tragedy, it engulfed the horizon. Beyond that, out of your line of vision, unfolded the national drama. Everyone felt concerned, hit by ricochets. Everyone wanted to know, was searching for answers. While they were looking for them, they stuffed you with painkillers. While they were tracking the attackers, they were putting you under anesthetic in the operating room. While the collective whole went from stupefaction to fear, from stupor to anger, victims had limbs amputated, others discovered that they would never walk again. A trapeze artist learned that she had lost the use of her hands. You didn't know if you would ever get a hard-on again.

After the events, you stayed cloistered in your burning hell for weeks, which turned into months. Compassionate, commiserating looks brought you back like an annoying backwash to your status as a star, a curiosity, a symbol. Please strike out whichever is not applicable. Not a victim like the others, in a world that nevertheless agrees to create them by spraying itself with pesticides, binging on additives, peppering itself with fine particles, harassing its women and its employees before they die on the roads or hang themselves. Not a victim like others, no. A survivor of the deadliest attacks perpetrated in France in seventy years. By hurting you, they hurt every one of us. Reactions about you went beyond solidarity. You are part of the besieged social body. Those who took care of you, ran into you, supported you, and helped you were attacked at the same time as you were. You were the paradigm of an embattled civilization, of assaulted freedom. You only understood this much later, even though since that November 13, 2015, people never stopped asking you ("Because you are a writer") if you were going to write *about* it.

No, you were going to write around it.

Write because you didn't have the choice, carried by a force that surpassed you. Write around it because you are a novelist and not a chronicler; because you can only craft a text by striving to make literature. Hence, neither testimony nor narrative. Invent something else. Form. Language. Dig deep. Have the boldness to allow yourself to lie, even by omission. If this meant putting your memories in order, that's nothing to you. You like to imagine. What's more, each time that you want to write down an event, a morsel of reality, you look for exactness, you get lost, lose your head. You would like to say everything, forget nothing, be panoramic and sweeping. As if you owed that minor detail to lived experience, the present author's homage to the world. You don't know how to report. Reporting bores you. Reporting imprisons you. Within the occurrence, the dateable, time spans, accuracy. Within facts. Which are factitious, fabricated. By language. From mental or geographical position. Which are by their nature rebellious. There is no objectivity about the real, even less so for the person who gets the urge to write it out. To hell with Stendhal's mirror! The real is but a view from the mind. Words do not betray or disfigure it. They construct something other, a parallel dimension. Sometimes, as pitfall or strategy, they rope in reality. Get passed off for it. Realism and accuracy are but distant cousins.

As a novelist, you are forever stuck between the heavy hammer of *kairos* and the anvil of your scruples.

"There's a bit of yourself in your novels, right? A bit of your life?"

A rhetorical question usually asked with a little smirk by somebody who won't be had. Yes, if you want (and many readers want that autobiographical dimension). If it makes you happy. You don't see what that changes in the reader's experience. The age demands *auto-fiction*. Hunt down the individual between the lines of the author. "Based on a true story" gives added value. The times call for voyeurism. However, if a novel isn't bigger than life, what good is it? Do you want the irrefutable? The AK-47 is an assault rifle invented by Mikhail Kalashnikov, of which there are many derivative models brought together under the name "Kalashnikov." You want some truth? Erwan Larher was wounded by a bullet shot from a Kalashnikov.[1] And afterward? Write a book starting with this? Three armed men entered the Bataclan and opened fire on the people inside. It would seem. You were inside. You were shot. You did not know that there were three assailants. You didn't see anything. The event that took place was one thousand five hundred events, and just as many states of mind. And for those who were outside, there were reports. Accounts.

---

[1] "The three weapons used in the concert hall came from three different countries. The first, brand name Zastava, was manufactured in Yugoslavia. This is the most readily available Kalashnikov on the black market. The second came from Bulgaria. And the third, named 'Type 56,' came from China. Able to fire 620 shots a minute in 'full-auto' mode, these models are the most sought after by terrorists, both for their ease of use and easy availability. Statistically, we can estimate that the number of Kalashnikov-variety assault rifles in the world varies from 50 to 200 million. In certain neighborhoods in France, their average price runs between 1,500 and 3,000 euros." Emmanuel Fansten and Willy Le Devin, "Attentats des policiers à toutes les preuves," *Libération.fr*, December 10, 2015.

"You must write about what you do not know," Eric Vuillard advised you[2] like an oracle as you came down in the early morning to write these lines, still wrapped up in your questions. Later on, an article in the *Le Clavier cannibale* would show you another way: "[Writing] isn't just about telling stories, but most of all about fitting sensations with a motor."

While writing your previous novel, you had given yourself a rule, written on standard letter-sized paper and taped on the wall over your computer screen: "No psychology!" Because you wanted neither testimony nor narrative, your goal for this new text, code-named *Project B*, repeated to any with the ears to hear it, would be to create a work of literature. If you could not achieve this, you would not send it to your editor.

A work of literature, and nothing else …

Break the rules. Get outside of your framework.

Panic.

You read novels that looked like "works of literature," soaking yourself in them. Discovering written works. Hunting down the voice, or voices, of your own text elsewhere. There you would find …

… sometimes …

… something of interest …

You would often be in admiration. At times you would grow weary.

You were a reader in need of a story.

---

[2] *Actes Sud*, July 14, 2016, p. 83.

A work of literature. Just who do you think you are, huh?

You owe the first two lines of this book to Emmanuel Régniez. One evening, dead tired, you took his *Notre château* from the mound at the foot of your bed to go to sleep. You opened it. "Everything started on a Thursday." You closed the book. You took your notebook and pen. You wrote. The ideas poured out. Make your work a realist tale? "I listened to rock"—now that's an acceptable beginning. The link with the Eagles of Death Metal is obvious. You would get there by taking a detour through your musical education. Perfect!

Yeah, right, a work of literature? You don't have the backbone for it.

June 2016. You had scribbled down a few dozen pages. You still hadn't found that leading theme. You thought your work was pathetic. Your editor asked you when you thought you would finish it. You told him that it would go fast, done before the end of the summer holidays. You didn't want this to drag on. You had started to write another novel, but that damnable *Project B* had shoved it aside. You said that it wouldn't be a very long text, most likely less than a hundred pages.

You jot down your thoughts in your notebook.

"Sequence of events?" If you followed this line, you'd fall into the swamp of a narrative. So work it out differently.

"What's the plot?" You needed a plot, right? You are a novelist who invents stories, not someone who turns his own story into a novel. You need your freedom. You didn't want to describe. The smell. The SCREAMING. Beyond words. Beyond imagination. You would have never gotten beyond the SCREAMING, no matter the writerly talent.

And then you tend to forget what has hurt you. Make it beautiful. Pretty it up. Be positive. The human brain is pretty damned well made! Yours is, at least. Pretty darned well wired. Because out of those weeks of pain, discomfort, and doubt only a mental pupa shell remains. And some ready-made sentences to drop during conversations. You know that it was painful, uncomfortable, but no lasting sore remains, no thorn in your daily life. Words. For others. You are programmed for the present. Made for the now. Sloughed-off skin—the needles, the pain waking you up in the middle of the night, the impossibility of sitting down, then of staying seated for more than ten minutes. Sloughed-off skin—bedsheets to change because the wound was infected and filling up with pus, the challenge of taking a shower, discouragement that gave rise to weeping, hours spent on the toilet waiting for ... Is it inescapable that torment and grief leave such foul traces, a scorched-earth landscape, and neurosis flowering on compost and dung?

Some know how to share their suffering, make you feel their torture, step inside their afflicted skin, make their pages ooze with it. Not you. Should you have forced yourself to? Gone deep inside yourself, a movement against the grain of nature? If the past still moves, that secret of the organic, food of zombies? Is it absolutely necessary to "let it out"? Maybe there is nothing inside, nothing to let out? You could have written this story as a drama. You have the technique to do that. It would have been easy to give yourself to tragedy and leave tear-soaked words. You wouldn't do that. You planned on writing a pastiche chapter full of pathos, defying all modesty, devil take restraint, a tale of woe to entertain yourself and your readers. To show them what fate they escaped. You would not do it.

A work of literature. What a joke!

You reminded yourself of a positive point when you were at wits' end. Writing about the Bataclan forced you to break free of your literary blinders. To draw yourself out of yourself, to confuse your questions and confound your doubts, you asked others to give you a text. Some who were close to you, others less so. Outside perspectives. Points of view that were different from your own. Many accepted.

By the end of July, wracked and blocked, you were suffocating under spineless, numb words and meandering sentences that were literally jumbled together topsy-turvy. The characters were there, of course. As well as the twists and turns. But what about the plot? The narrative progression? Can you write a book without that? What will become of our hero? We already know that he makes it out alive. Is it possible to make a story that doesn't go from Point A to Point B hold together? Because if this one has a beginning, it doesn't have an end. Whereas every book has a last page, right?

And then in the middle of the summer, the ending occurred to you. The most beautiful one imaginable. The ending to end all endings. Then the words raised their heads, suddenly coherent, and the sentences found their way. There is a Point A, a Point B, and something between them—a work of literature. You can be really bombastic sometimes!

5

I WENT INTO THE CONCERT HALL. Familiar sensations. Immediate bliss. A rock concert. I smiled. I was well.

From then on, it was no longer your story. Not *only* your story. Or rather it is my story, because I am the one telling it.

It is no longer only my story. It is also yours, Iblis.

You were afraid. How couldn't you have been, with a belt of explosives around your waist? Did your commanders let you hope that you were going to make it out? "Fire into the crowd, take hostages, and ask for a plane ready to take off." Or rather, "Go in, slaughter, get out, then meet at the agreed site for your escape." Did you have any strategy other than to *put on a show*? Had your chiefs wiped out the future: "Go in, fire into the crowd, then improvise"? It was cool on paper. In front of the Bataclan Café, weighed down with three-and-a-half pounds of triacetone triperoxide, plus nuts, bolts, nails, and batteries, you were afraid.

Getting ready was exhilarating. You knew you were going to hit it big, 9–11 style. You were too young to understand, but they had told you the story, like they told me the story of the Battle of Poitiers when I was a child. You were proud to have been chosen for this mission.

You would be the harbinger of shock and awe. You were going to turn reality into a blockbuster, throw the newspapers into a panic, horrify the populace, shatter the French Republic, throw oil on the geopolitical bonfire. Extravagant staging and an immediate impact. At the worst, or the best, you would be a martyr. Unlike Efrit, sweating next to you in the seat of a stolen car, you never believed in those stories of virgins and Heaven. He never let a prayer slip by. Before, you would easily say that you felt "zero-level Muslim." You were a knight. A righter of wrongs. A redeemer. You were going to avenge those innocents slaughtered by the West. To finally act, rather than survive in a society that barely tolerated you, checked your papers due to your race, looked askance at your wife who wears a veil and, unlike you, speaks with a slight accent. And not with an accent from the French countryside. You imagined your name etched forever in history. Except right then, it was no longer about getting ready, about fiery speeches, or laughing about the great trick you were getting ready to play on those infidel dogs. Your mouth was dry, and your stomach in knots. You were afraid.

You looked out the car window. A lanky silhouette in a black leather coat lit up a cigarette, then, motorcycle helmet in hand, walked windblown across the boulevard. You guessed that the silhouette was heading to the concert. *BANG!*

There were four of you in the car. Three were soon going to pounce to kill in the name of a God who hadn't done much for you until then. The outgoing, the righteous, and the idiot. Or were there two who were outgoing, and one righteous one? Weren't each of you a bit of all of that at the same time? It is very romantic to find three qualifying elements when there are three characters. *The Good, the Bad, and the Ugly* have done more damage to literature than we'd like to admit.

You were thrilled. You were going to act. Finally. After months of training, dangerous border crossings, and weeks hiding out. After living like rats, looking over your shoulder, trusting no one, lying to your friends and family.

Were you thrilled? You had to stay cold. Methodical. Concentrated. It stank in the car—sour sweat. And your black clothes did not smell laundry fresh. Saala had bad breath. May not one grain of sand ... A heroic cop, the hall not laid out like on the blueprints—it would be full, which changed everything. A stuck door. Or Efrit who could lose it ... You could manipulate Saala to your delight. You thought he was an idiot. You weren't far from despising him, but that's how it was in your neighborhood soccer team. You can't be friends with everybody. At least he had the balls to be there.

At the time when you met him, he would constantly watch videos of Westerners getting their heads cut off on his telephone. While smoking a cigarette, while talking, during meals. All the time. He was convinced that Paris was "the capital of abominations and perversions." He gladly drank vodka, and he didn't like blacks. In the training camp in Syria, it pissed him off that the

Sudanese, the Malians, and the Nigerians didn't keep their undies on to take a shower. You often noticed how he couldn't stop himself from ogling their long, plump dicks. When a patrol caught a Somalian deserter, Saala asked to be allowed to cut off his head. On the first try, he got the guy's ear and a part of his scalp. Everybody laughed at him, especially when the instructor said that it was because he had closed his eyes right before the blow hit. Saala was furious. The prisoner bellowed and was spewing blood, but you all didn't give a damn. You all were laughing too hard, even if you yourself weren't feeling so well. Saala picked up his saber again, all surly. The blade sliced through the air and made a huge "crack." Saala fell on his ass, provoking the deepest glee. The cutting edge must have got stopped by a vertebra or something like that. The prisoner's head was dangling on one side. He looked utterly amazed at what was happening to him. Saala was mortified. You vomited in your scarf. The instructor raised his hand while looking at you. Everyone stopped laughing. He commanded you to pull the blade out and finish cutting that fucking head off. You must have had to pull yourself together three times. They sent you back to Europe two days later.

You were afraid. You would have liked to open the door and run away. Death was no longer just a word. If the Paris Saint-Germain soccer team were to win the Champions League, you would not feel the excitement of their road to victory. (Nevertheless, you dreamed of seeing them beat Barcelona.) You would no longer see your wife or your daughter. Or your friends at the bar. Or your parents, always a source of shame for you, who kowtowed and kept a low profile, simply happy to be allowed to live in France. Would they be proud of you, those who had taught you to never make yourself stand out, not make waves, always say "Hello" and "Thank you"? These basic questions tightened the jaws of the vise that was gnawing at your guts, leaving you breathless. Are we doing this or what?

You were afraid. There was no going back anymore. You had hit a dead end. You regretted it. Efrit was praying next to you, eyes half-shut and quiet, but his lips moving. He spoke Arabic. You didn't. That was a problem in Syria. The Isis combatants did not trust you, or anyone from France. They were afraid of double agents and traitors. They restricted you to the lowest tasks. You did not fight over there. You trained, and you did manual labor. Guarding prisoners. It was hot. You were as bored as you were in your suburban apartment. You were bored a lot in your life. You never felt you had found your place. You were never sure there was one for you. You played soccer, as a sweeper, always second-guessing yourself and not aggressive enough, according to your coach. You defended the youngsters at your school and in your neighborhood. You half-heartedly sold a few bars of bad hash. You were a pretty good student, but you were also bored in the classroom. As Amir, your soccer team's goalkeeper, who could have gone pro if he hadn't been so crazy, used to say: "An Arab is either the best or the worst student. Being average means nothing." You graduated, then got your vocational degree. You started to work with a badly paid, short-term contract. You were bored with your colleagues. The days before and after matches you would talk with some of them, even if you really did not have the time. "Hey, you guys, this job isn't gonna get done by itself!" your manager would shout as soon as the break was over. The bastard used a stopwatch. He said he didn't have the choice. So you would go back to work, back to work that meant nothing. Preparing orders in a huge hangar. No room for error, because you were graded. It was freezing in winter, and you cooked in summer. And the sound of the robots. The sound of the conveyor belts. The sound of the trolleys. And the end of the day, a migraine plus commute time to head home plus no bars in that industrial zone where everyone keeps to their side of the tracks. When it came to going on strike because of on-the-job accidents, or temps, or longer breaks (you don't remember anymore), there were barely ten strikers. And six got fired. You were right to keep a low profile. On the Internet, you discovered that your company's boss, an American, was the third wealthiest man in the world.

You were only tolerated when you went out into the city. Certain gestures and tones of voice traced out an otherness that you were eventually required to embody. You didn't feel any different from the pale faces that got into the Pacha Club when you still had to wait outside. You didn't feel any different from the assholes laughing at the next table sitting next to dolled-up babes. Except that you wondered where they found such friends? How did they create a group of friends? Had they grown up together? Went to school together? They would talk about going on holiday as a group. You had only left on holiday once, at the age of twelve, to the country of your roots. The youngsters who were your age, even your cousins, left you by yourself for a month. No place for you. Nowhere a place for you. And there was always this sneaking, sticky, sinister feeling that nothing would change, that everything was already set and played out ahead of time. Some could sneak in between the lines, but either they would switch camps, like Djamel Debbouze or Omar Sy, or they would be lambasted and trashed. From Samy Naceri to Karim Benzema. Or Samir Nasri, who no longer got selected for the French soccer team because he opened his big mouth too much.

You had to make yourself small, like your parents. Say "Hello" and "Thank you."

And maybe the Palestinians should say thank you to Israel? Should the civilians who died under the West's bombs in Syria and those who mourned them say thank you? The feeling of injustice stoked your bravery. You were dying from the heat. Soon you would quite simply die. Dying was an idea. A word. A scene from a film with Bruce Willis or Russell Crowe. In those action films that you loved (like me), even when they died, they didn't *really* die.

Could we have been pals, you and me? Played soccer or had some drinks together? Talked about classic French films like *Un Singe en hiver* or *Le Magnifique*? You knew all of Belmondo's lines by heart. You were a fan of his and could imitate him perfectly, as your neighbors told us. They couldn't believe it, camera close-up shot. Iblis, so helpful, so kind, so discreet. Are you sure we're talking about the same Iblis? So, he was on drugs? Yes, it's the same Iblis, and no, no traces of drugs.

EXCLUSIVE!
THOSE CLOSE TO THE TERRORIST SPEAK!

We did not see you much at the mosque. You were not one of the firm believers. Your brothers and your parents thought that you had been doing better for a while. They did not know it, but you had given your life a meaning. That was calming and encouraging, right? At least it was until now, because that death strapped to your torso is starting to show its weight and weigh you down. Why is it taking so long? Open the door and run away. That would be so easy. You put your hand on the door handle.

"*Allahu akbar*, people will still be talking about us in one thousand years," Saala stated with conviction, turning toward you.

You let the door handle go. You were going to make a name for yourself. The hour of glory. You could not stop yourself from letting out a loud fart. Efrit scowled at you while continuing to intone his prayers.

6

YOU WENT INTO THE CONCERT HALL.

On the stage, a young woman thanked the audience, who applauded rather warmly. The lights went back on. I had got there right at the end of the opening act. I headed to the bar before it got inaccessible and ordered a beer. While waiting to be served, I scanned the surroundings trying to find familiar faces. I had worked almost ten years in the music industry and go to so many concerts that I usually run into at least one acquaintance. Not that night. I must be getting on. My well-being was not improved by the high price of the beer.

The roadies were busy changing the set. Unplugging the microphones and speakers, rolling up cables, and putting equipment in flight cases, then the cases in the tour bus, taping picks on the microphone stands and the set list to the floor in front of the monitor speakers. I had gone through the same motions at the start of my professional life, most likely with that same, slightly haughty expression of laid-back pride that says, "Yeah, I am also part of the show. I'm on stage." (Even if it's just to plug in jacks and tune the guitars.)

I knew my day of glory as an assistant stage manager on November 15 at the Olympia concert hall. The Innocents were on stage. I was backstage right. All of a sudden, Jipé Nataf's guitar strap detached. He kept playing and singing while throwing desperate glances my way. I was waiting for the general manager, Vince, or one of the group's regular roadies to rush to his aid. Nothing. So I bolted into the stage lights, shaking and panic-stricken, and reattached the strap. I will always remember Jipé's grateful look and smile. Later, I would repulse him by bluntly stating that I didn't dig their recorded music, but they blew me away live. After a second of silence, he burst out laughing. "Well at least you don't pull any punches!" Above all I was a stupid little fucker.

My (bad) beer in hand, I positioned myself to the right of the mixing board surrounded by a metal barricade, behind which the Eagles of Death Metal's sound engineer was already enthroned, aware of his importance—the pudgy, tattooed overlord of a 44-square-foot kingdom. All the prouder when he was joined by a tantalizing sex bomb done up in high rock 'n' roll style, with tattoos, piercings, Doc Martens, and a tartan mini-skirt over destroyed stockings. It is easy to understand why that is where the sound is best at a concert. If the energy takes me, I get closer to the stage. With some groups, it is unthinkable to not be in the front rows, where the pleasure becomes physical, where bodies take over, or you jump, move, dance, and sweat together. During one of my first concerts—Simple Minds in Brest—I lost a kind of moccasin in the human tsunami that washed me to the left. I found it by miracle when the glob of bodies flowed back to the right.

Since then, I have carefully chosen my footwear when I go to a rock concert—often savage and even rambunctious. Nothing too fragile or too delicate. Generally, I slide on my Doc Martens or, like that night, my cowboy boots. Tennis shoes are not very rock, except for Converse All Stars, punked up by the Ramones. But can you name a shoe that is less comfortable, without even talking about the appearance? And here's a "coming out" that many purists will never forgive: I don't like The Ramones. On the other hand, I love shoes. I have a dozen pairs of them, all of the highest quality. I spend a lot on them, choose only ones that will never go out of fashion and have a timeless elegance (or at least that's what I would like to think), and I keep them a long time. Those boots have been through quite a few concerts.

I leaned up against one of the columns supporting the balcony, in one of those states of worldly bliss that lets thoughts come all by themselves, to gallivant in your skull and give birth to others that you can neither control nor critique.

I was feeling good. With my people.

To my right, people were going up and down the three steps that lead to the dance floor (or to the bar, depending on which direction you were taking). I was observing, a smile on my face, relaxed. I love that mood. My brethren believers and I had come together in the same spirit, ready to join in fellowship. Happy. They were *mes semblables, mes frères*. We were united by rock. A feel-good affinity. You can find a certain photo on the Internet taken from the stage right before the concert. I have downloaded it and look at from time to time to salute those friends I have never met. Joyful faces, devil hands raised high, smiles. Bonds. Real lives and real people, with stories and hopes, secrets and foibles, and generosity. There was a friend, a neighbor, your eldest daughter's dance teacher, the owner of the local wine shop. Real laughter and friends and lovers. You can make out my silhouette, in the background, against the column. I sometimes wonder who in this photo might ... Anyway, you know what I wonder. Almost all the victims were younger than me.

The dance floor was filling up. Some elbow others out of the way to reach a better place. I could make out the old-school diehards with skull and cross bones and weathered leather, with mutton chops and faded Jon Spencer Blues Explosion or AC/DC T-shirts. A minority among the hipsters sporting more or less the same look: carefully trimmed beards, hair cut to reveal ears and the backs of their necks, long hair strands impeccably cared for, pants that were a bit too short. I tried to imagine them without that studied appearance, enjoyed the result, wondered why they wished to look like their neighbor, and smiled at the not very good jokes told by a small group next to me. Two tattooed forty-somethings stopped not far away. I heard a few words in German. A girl walks behind me, laughing in her phone: "Where are you? I can't see you ... Raise

your hands … No, I can't see anything. I'm too short."
I showed her where her friend was, whose hand I saw
raised in the middle of the dance floor. She thanked me.
Are they dead now? But if I had not helped that young
girl, she might have asked her friend to join her at the bar.
And that way, would her chances of buying it have been
higher? Are those hipsters that I (kindly) upbraided in
my inner mind and who were right in the middle of the
passage also dead? Just wounded? With a bullet in your
body, you do not think any more about how you look.

Impatience was rising in the concert hall. The room
started clapping. This big, stoked, quivering body wanted
its fix. Latecomers cut a path toward the stage, plastic
glasses of beer in hand. Probability they were hit: very
high. Conversations got less lively, eyes turned toward
those orphan instruments and the mute speakers. The
crowd drew together.

Lights out. Shouts of joy. Cheers. I smiled. I was well.
With my people.

The group stepped on stage. Devil hands lifted to
heaven all over the room. First riffs, first feedback, rock,
energy, togetherness. So fucking good!

At 9:40, or 9:42, or 9:47—they couldn't even fucking
agree on that—the sound of firecrackers. The musicians
froze, then ran off the stage. Shouts and motion. Those
weren't firecrackers. "Get down! Get down!"

I threw myself to the floor.

This is where this book begins. Unless it began without
warning me.

As Seen from Outside: III

I don't know how it started any more—how I learned
that Paris had been handed over to murderers, like
in that song by Reggiani, "The Wolves Have Entered
Paris." The other day, somebody told me that some
high-level experts, probably American (there are no
more experts in France; we'd know about it if there
were), had found with absolutely certainty that a
novel with the word "Wolf" in its title stood a one-
hundred-percent chance of being crowned with
popular success. Here's your proof: *Wolfering Heights,
Remembrance of Wolves Past, Gone with the Wolves,
Marguerite Doesn't Like Her Wolves...*

Which goody-two-shoes media snitch first reported
that the evening of November 13 had turned into
overblown horror? Had I heard the news through a cell
phone alert, or by following my Facebook thread? This
is how we all are solicited at every moment by news
so equally pointless and provocative that it all gets
mixed up and chewed up, like a pack of wolves eager
for blood and sensationalism.

From the first shootings on the café patios, I was
stuck to the TV screen, totally stunned and benumbed,
just as useless as the journalists reporting live on-site.
There was something rather funny that happened
when the Bataclan daze hit. Rushed journalists started
talking about "The Eagles." The Eagles? The ones with

the two-necked guitars who sang "Hotel California"—
one of the few songs I know how to play on the
guitar? And thanks to which I was able to seduce
dozens of Norwegian girls in the July of my nineteenth
year, on beaches where the sun set when I would get
down to business?

The Eagles got back together? They were playing at
the Bataclan?

It took a few passing minutes to correct those
panic-induced blunders. All sources agreed that the
concert hall was, at that very moment, the scene of
an unprecedented slaughter in Paris. And then, once
again very quickly, there was a Facebook alert. It
was Erwan's girlfriend Jeanne who had just created
a group to tell us, the new charter members of
the Horrified Club and me, that Erwan was in the
audience at the Bataclan for the Eagles of Death
Metal concert, that he had left without his cell phone,
and that she would notify the group of any news as
soon as possible. As soon as she had any. A bone-
chilling, unforeseeable shock. Which grew deeper and
added to the collective shock. Out of fear-induced
disbelief, I quickly brought up Erwan's Facebook page
and his last post. Full of the ecstasy of a guy free as
the wind, who loves you, who goads you and is going
to a good old rock 'n' roll concert where he plans to

pogo like a madman. Confirming his presence right in the middle of that mindless butchery orchestrated by barbarians, and whose drama was starting to be broadcast on television. As the minutes and the hours passed, I stayed glued to the Facebook thread and to the screens of the news channels. Starting from shots fired, we went to an organized gang of fundamentalists hopped up on God only knows what kind of insanity and set on making as many victims as possible. I told myself that with my buddy's look, he wasn't going to last long. With his lanky, long-haired air of Jesus of Nazareth ... If those fuckers fell on him, there were only two solutions: either they blow him away or they get converted to Christianity.

More time passed, with shovel-loads of anxiety, and more participants in the Horrified Club, and still no reassuring news from Jeanne. But there was a reassuring side, all the same. In the fleeting creation of that Facebook group. As if Jeanne were taking care of us, soothing our stupor, that she could relieve us of at any time.

After dread and anxiety, anger had now taken me over. Anger against those barbarians—what were they thinking? Anger against my country, unable to protect its youth—so you can head to Paris with Kalashnikovs and open fire at random, or not necessarily at random

but at anyone whatsoever? Anger against Erwan,
who left without his cell phone—as if that would
have changed anything. And once again anger against
Erwan because I knew that, once he got out of that
hell, he wouldn't even be angry at them. He would
keep on looking at the world with his cyber-sprite face
and swinging satchel bag. And that's for the best.

I don't know if that anger reassured me, proved to
me that he was alive and was going to get out of that
shithole alive. But I couldn't stop saying this to my
lover: "I am sure he won't even hate them for it!"

I spent the evening with her, in the 12th
arrondissement of Paris. We must have been on the
first-aid trajectory—at the same time, emergency
workers must have been rushing from all over the
place—because there was an uninterrupted ballet of
sirens all night long. Not the kind of Busby Berkeley
choreography where you dive one by one into the
calm, shimmering waters of an Olympic pool, but a
siren dance that bursts your eardrums and wears on
your nerves well after the show is over. How do you
get over that? How do you swim up to the surface?
Then we learned that there were hostages. I wanted
to go get a loudspeaker and shout out to those
cowards, "Free Erwan Larher! You cannot make
him part of the dead poets' society! He hasn't even

published a poetry collection!" In the end, no hostage would be killed, as if their rain of hatred had dissuaded the criminals from continuing their slaughter, or as if it was just easier to shoot people in the back and by surprise than when they were standing right next to you. Cowards. Cowards who put our own cowardice to the test. Nobody talks about it, but what kind of society, what kind of religion can stand being represented by such cowards? They were above all else cowards, and those media assholes who were going to broadcast their portraits throughout their newsfeeds to make them erotic, to make them ready-made icons for all the addle-brained losers of this world who dream of wreaking vengeance on their own failures by taking down others.

How can you swim up to the surface? Sometimes I feel like a Busby Berkeley swimmer who touches the bottom of the pool and rises back up to see that we have changed, we have regressed from a '30s musical to a stark, Paul Verhoeven-style horror film.

I don't remember if it was during the night or in the early morning when Jeanne notified us that Erwan was safe and sound, that he was being taken care of at the Créteil hospital, and that it was not too serious.

Not too serious? Is that what we've come to? I just know that he won't even hate them for it!

7

HE WAS SCARED. Wanted to piss. He wanted to run away. That belt of explosives was getting heavy and making it hard to move. It stunk in the car, and stupid fucking Efrit could not stop praying. At the steering wheel, Shaitan received a text message and gave the signal. Finally!

Here we go!

Iblis got out of the car. Stopped for a second to feel the fresh air on his face. "What the hell are you doing?" Saala shouted at him. He calmly took his post across from the Bataclan Café and opened fire, one bullet at a time. Efrit stayed on the Passage Saint-Pierre-Amelot to surprise the public that would soon escape from the emergency exits. That was the plan: to put a stranglehold on the crowd. Iblis headed to the concert hall entrance and shot a security guard. Firing at anything that moved. Sweaty hands, calm nevertheless. He could see himself being seen, as the scene played out before his eyes—the horrified gazes, the spurting blood. Huge. Invincible. Fear swallowed up by almighty power.

They went up the stairs. No one behind the coat check counter. Iblis pushed the swinging doors to go into the concert hall and took snipe shots at the darkness, full on automatic. Saala headed right. Bodies fell. SCREAMS. A burst of gunfire to the left. Efrit must have got in, thought Iblis, loading a new clip into his weapon. He went to semi-automatic firing mode and charged toward the dance floor, blowing away stunned spectators. *BANG!* *BANG!* A lot of bodies on the floor. Rushing all around. He shot anyone that moved. One shot to the right, one to the left. SCREAMS. The mixing board to his right, overturned behind the metal barrier. *BANG!* *BANG!* Adrenaline. Sweat oozing down his neck. Delight. Elation. Omnipotence.

Vengeance.

Firing, he walked down the three steps that led to the dance floor. One shot to the left, one to the right. Bodies everywhere, tangled together, wailing, moaning, cowering. He was going to finish off a wounded victim at his feet, when all of a sudden the house lights went up. So he went into automatic firing mode, raised his weapon, and sprayed bullets on the panic, the shock, and the SCREAMS.

8

WONDERING IF THOSE ARE FIRECRACKERS ...
Is that part of the show, or ... "Get down! Get
down!" (Who are those heroes who scream that order
while under fire?) You threw yourself to the floor.

Sound of firecrackers you turn your head to the left
sparks falling bits of plasters is this part of the show or ...
"Get down! Get down!" You threw yourself to the floor.

Sounds of firecrackers you saw one of the forbidden
unprotected musicians on the stage two others made a
run for it this is not part of the show "Get down! Get
down!" You threw yourself to the floor.

It was 9:40 pm according to certain sources; however,
the last telephone conversation from Shaitan's cell phone,
later dropped in a garbage can, was at 9:42 pm, and then
the surveillance cameras on the street confirmed that the
assault started at 9:47 pm.

Who cares?

Inside, time had stopped. Reality twisted into the
surreal. The outside faded away, and the interior became
everything, that moment the whole universe, nothing
else, no elsewhere because there was no way out.

Hyper-horror is a crack in space-time.

Firecrackers "Get down! Get down!" You threw

yourself to the floor. Everything got jumbled up, mixed up, Sigolène, sparks and flashes of shouts the smell of heat and gunpowder and that horrible dry dull sound kept popping. The sound of war, yes, war is that sound, no doubt about it. Oliver and his mole traps, you were on the ground, in the fetal position, what the fuck?

You sidled up to the barrier that cut the kingdom of peril off from the sound mixer, the shouts, fuck, the shouts! And the deadly staccato that wouldn't stop, the shouts, the sound of racing, war, the unthinkable, the shock, the SCREAMS, I was in the middle of the action, I saw them trying to run away, I pulled the trigger, BANG! BANG! They fell, they screamed, was Saala screaming too while emptying his weapon on these begging, frightened hipsters, who were pushing each other, trampling each other, falling haphazard onto each other? I was almighty, I was vengeance, I was a hero, I was Bruce Willis, I could ace every level of *Call of Duty*, this shit is lit! I had already seen myself scoring the winning goal in the final of the Champions League, and it wasn't this good. Being with girls had never been this good. Empty clip. Efrit looked at me. He blew up a head at point-blank range with a big grin. That guy was a sicko.

You were vengeance. You were Iblis. You wanted to shout your own name. So they would know. So they would remember. Were you a hero? Were you a coward? You were wholly and completely there, for the last time.

I got down on the floor. Smashed up against the barricade. The shots were getting closer. Some from then on were single shots, I thought. *BANG! BANG!* I couldn't see anything. I could hear war. Panic. Sonic apocalypse. The smell was aggressive too, bitter and sweetish, blood and gunpowder, guts, even shouts smell like death, wisps of shouts, orders, Don't move! *BANG! BANG!* I told you not to move!

Was I scared? Most likely, but that wasn't terror. I was trying to disappear into the metal barrier, to melt into it. I understood that I could not slide under it to hide out under the mixing board. Other bodies lying down, behind me, next to me. Whispers between bursts of gunfire, between attack waves. I couldn't see anything. I didn't know what was going on, just that we were under attack. I would have liked to meld into the ground. Become the floorboards. I was staring at my end. For the first time.

The end.

No more me.

I, dissolved.

Me, dissolved.

How could the world keep on going if I were no longer there? It couldn't outlive me, right? If I died, reality would die, you would all die. I had heard my maternal grandmother say that she wanted to pass away, that she was too tired to live. It took too much out of her. She wasn't interested in it anymore. How is it that, one day, you just stop wanting to live? That you could grow weary of everything? Really, of everything? Like an album you've listened to too much, or a shirt you've worn too many times. Can you just stop putting up with life? There I was, in my becoming-floor, my becoming-barricade. I don't know if I was scared. I was not praying, but I did not want to die. That's for sure.

I wanted to not die.

(I was thinking that, in dreams, you wake up just before it happens.)

Bursts of gunfire, warfare, SCREAMS, my disbelief, my stupefaction. *BANG! BANG!* I couldn't see anything. I couldn't turn my head. I could hear *BANG! BANG!* Don't move! *BANG! BANG!* Shut up! *BANG! BANG!* (Did I have something to atone for?) *BANG! BANG! BANG!*

You were shooting your suffering and your jealousy. You were shooting your unquenched desires and your frustration. You were shooting like Johnny Rambo or Al Pacino. You were shooting without thinking, without morality. You were shooting because no one had ever shot you—if not, Iblis, I swear that you would have opened that car door and split. You were shooting because you were there and you had to see it through. You were shooting your boredom and your parents' servility, shooting Mathieu Valbuena, Barack Obama, Shimon Peres, Didier Deschamps, *Charlie Hebdo*. You were shooting your bruised destiny, shooting injustice, shooting infidels, shooting all those who would hurt those you call your brothers. You were shooting in rage with clenched teeth. Or with a laugh. You shot when a cell phone rang, when a head poked up. Emperor Nero of your gruesome, pathetic pandemonium, armed guard in the service of a twisted *Lex talionis*. You wiped out a possible neighbor, a possible friend of a friend. You wanted action? Well, you got some! People screaming, blood spurting. Wailing, falling bodies. Shapeless magma. You opened fire. Shadows tried to flee while you were reloading, but they weren't fast enough. You shot them in the back, in the legs. You were a knight, an avenger. You liquidated the bouncer who blocked the door to you, the ever-so-slightly racist cop who busted you for having a small slab of hash, that guy you once heard in Toulon, with his shitty accent, telling his buddy over a pastis that the only good towel-head is a dead towel-head. Those bourgeois you were raining your 600-bullet-a-minute hatred down upon didn't know that that kind of racism existed. Those people, those white folks, screaming and drowning in their own blood, those people you had turned into enemies, notions, targets, outlets for your erratic scorn. They didn't know because racism is like taking a bullet. It's something you have experience to understand. They didn't know and would have thought you were going too far if you were to tell them everything. If you had the words to do so. If they would even speak to you. But no, they stick with each other on classy café patios, they dance with each other under the watch of black security guards, and they fuck each other, forgetful or ignorant of tortured North African freedom fighters, and the dead of Charonne. You didn't even know what Charonne means. Or the Sykes-Picot Accords. Or what Pan-Arabism is. You didn't know who Suleiman the

Magnificent, Mustafa Kemal, Ibn Tufayl, or Avicenna were. You didn't have any political awareness, any roots in the past. You were just a finger on a trigger in the permanent present of postmodernity. You were just the newsfeed on 24-hour non-stop news channels. You were Columbine High come to Europe, imported by ignorance and greed. You leaped from the pages of Debord and Bourdieu, of Bruno Etienne and de Tocqueville, but thought doesn't come across well on the screen, thought doesn't make you money, doesn't win you votes. Thought enlightens, but some people need monsters lurking in the darkness to sell their show.

You were nothingness, the apocalypse. You had never read the Koran (as opposed to Efrit, who insulted his victims in Arabic); you had never read anything in fact.
    You were nothing.
    So you shot.
    To become something.

From 9:40, or 9:42, or 9:47 pm on, this story was no longer my own. Because you had turned me into a barricade, a floor, an animal, and none of those things has a story.

As Seen from Outside: IV

Romain Renard Euuh. ça va?
J'aime · Répondre · 13 novembre 2015, 22:40

Anne Icart Erwan ?
J'aime · Répondre · 13 novembre 2015, 22:46

Sandra Reinflet Putain EL, ça va ? (flippe / pensée pour toi)
J'aime · Répondre · ⭕1 · 13 novembre 2015, 22:47

Vania Pagano Oh! Espérant que tu ailles bien.
J'aime · Répondre · 13 novembre 2015, 22:47

Eloïse Lièvre Merde Erwan, tu es là-bas!
J'aime · Répondre · 13 novembre 2015, 22:52

Mathieu Reumaux Habla?
Voir la traduction
J'aime · Répondre · 13 novembre 2015, 22:52

Esther Launey Allo ???? Ça va ???
J'aime · Répondre · 13 novembre 2015, 22:53

Romain Renard Um, you ok?
Like • Comment • November 13, 2015 at 10:40 PM

Anne Icart Erwan?
Like • Comment • November 13, 2015 at 10:46 PM

Sandra Reinflet Fuck EL, u ok? (freaking out/thinking of you)
Like • Comment • ⭕1 • November 13, 2015 at 10:47 PM

Vania Pagano Oh! Hope you are well.
Like • Comment • November 13, 2015 at 10:47 PM

Eloïse Lièvre Shit Erwan, you're there!
Like • Comment • November 13, 2015 at 10:52 PM

Mathieu Reumaux Habla?
See the translation
Like • Comment • November 13, 2015 at 10:52 PM

Esther Launey Hello???? You OK???
Like • Comment • November 13, 2015 at 10:53 PM

Delphine Bertholon Oui please Erwan, donne des news (ça a pété aussi en bas de chez moi, je flippe à mort).
J'aime · Répondre · 13 novembre 2015, 22:55

Sandrine Lebars Erwan donne de tes nouvelle s'il te plaît s'il te plaît !!!!!!
J'aime · Répondre · 13 novembre 2015, 22:56

Cedric Fabre Erwan !
J'aime · Répondre · 13 novembre 2015, 23:01

Franck Courtès Le premier qui a des nouvelles d'Erwan peut il informer les autres svp?
J'aime · Répondre · 🕙 10 · 13 novembre 2015, 23:04

Sandrine Lebars J'ai pas son numéro moi quelque a essayé de l'appeler ???
J'aime · Répondre · 13 novembre 2015, 23:05

    Franck Courtès oui il répond pas
    J'aime · Répondre · 13 novembre 2015, 23:06

    Votre réponse...

Delphine Bertholon Yes, pleeez Erwan, give some newz (shots downstairs from me too. Totally freaking out).
Like · Comment · November 13, 2015 at 10:55 PM

Sandrine Lebars Erwan, give us some news, please, please!!!!!!
Like · Comment · November 13, 2015 at 10:56 PM

Cedric Fabre Erwan!
Like · Comment · November 13, 2015 at 11:01 PM

Franck Courtès The first one who gets news about Erwan tells the others, pls?
Like · Comment · 🕙 10 · November 13, 2015 at 11:04 PM

Sandrine Lebars I don't have his number. Has someone tried to call him???
Like · Comment · November 13, 2015 at 11:05 PM

    Franck Courtès Tried, no anwer
    Like · Comment · November 13, 2015 at 11:06 PM

    Your comment

Cedric Fabre Il y a qui d'autre avec lui, quelquun sait ?
J'aime · Répondre · 13 novembre 2015, 23:06

Sigolène Dunmassifduchili Erwan n'a pas son portable avec lui. Personne n'a de nouvelle.
J'aime · Répondre · 🔘 1 · 13 novembre 2015, 23:06

Cedric Fabre On a son numéro, oui... On ose pas appeler.
J'aime · Répondre · 13 novembre 2015, 23:07

Cedric Fabre Parano totale...
J'aime · Répondre · 13 novembre 2015, 23:07

Sigolène Dunmassifduchili Pas la peine d'appeler, il n'a pas son téléphone.
J'aime · Répondre · 13 novembre 2015, 23:07

Peggy Martineau ??
J'aime · Répondre · 13 novembre 2015, 23:09

Séverine Laus-Toni L'angoisse totale.......
J'aime · Répondre · 13 novembre 2015, 23:12

Judith Azoulay Erwan donne nous des news...des que tu peux, jet en prie
J'aime · Répondre · 13 novembre 2015, 23:20

Cedric Fabre Who else is with him? Anybody know?
Like • Comment • November 13, 2015 at 11:06 PM

Sigolène Dunmassifduchili Erwan does not have his cell on him. No news from anybody.
Like • Comment • 🔘 1 • November 13, 2015 at 11:06 PM

Cedric Fabre Got his number ... don't dare call.
Like • Comment • November 13, 2015 at 11:07 PM

Cedric Fabre Total freakout ...
Like • Comment • November 13, 2015 at 11:07 PM

Sigolène Dunmassifduchili No need to try. He doesn't have his phone.
Like • Comment • November 13, 2015 at 11:07 PM

Peggy Martineau ???
Like • Comment • November 13, 2015 at 11:09 PM

Séverine Laus-Toni Totally stressing out
Like • Comment • November 13, 2015 at 11:12 PM

Judith Azoulay Erwan, give us some news as soon as you can, please!
Like • Comment • November 13, 2015 at 11:20 PM

9

CHAOS? HELL? JUST WORDS. That cannot flesh out the situation. Only a calm, polite present can be described on the spot, tamed by words. The experience of brutality and cruelty can only be expressed in the past, emptied of its horror, checked by memory's gaps and holes, kept at a distance by endlessly pared-down and mutually supportive sentences, adjectives, vocabulary. Which, between focusing in and backing off, you must set in place to render terror a thing of the past.

Chaos. Hell. Those are words used from the outside, in that outer world sucked into the vortex of extreme violence—that world that you were not going to see anymore. At least not with the same eyes.

You were thinking about neither chaos nor hell, because you weren't thinking anymore. Were you afraid? Possibly. Or rather so beyond fear that you were no longer afraid. Had to save your skin. Curled up, in the fetal position, against the barricade. You couldn't see anything, head slid under the black cloth covering the metal. Had to save your skin by getting small, invisible, in the uproar and frenzy, in the hot stink of guts and gunpowder. In the foreground, a blast nearby. Followed by a scream. Then another blast, closer this time. Another scream. War.

Death. Had to get out of this. Holding onto survival. You were nothing but survival. Had to shrink down. Had to disappear. Were you a coward? A blast, this time really close. A scream. A blast. A boom. Dry. Iblis was getting closer. Execution. All around, still chaos (or hell?), but you could only hear the single shots popping off, coming toward you. Helplessness. Your whole being relaxed. A coward? Maybe. Is that question asked so close to death? A blast, this time just behind you.

You would not get out of this.

A .30 caliber bullet shot at point-blank range enters the flesh at around 2,300 feet per second, or more than 1,550 miles an hour. Around twice the speed of sound.

So the .30 caliber bullet most likely entered your body before you heard the blast.

You shrieked with a jolt. Play dead, you thought, fuck, this pain, he knows you're not dead he's right over you fuck, the pain, GODDAMMIT, he's going to finish you off with one bullet

in the head.
With one bullet in the head
That's for sure.
Suspension of time (yes, it can stop).

You were calm.
You were going to die.

Suspension of time (yes, it can stop).
   You were calm. You were going to die.
   With a bullet to the head. Why would he spare you?
   You did not see your life flash by.
   You were calm despite the physical pain.
   It's going to be quick, you told yourself. Too quick.
   I hope it won't hurt. I hope it happens fast.

When the topic comes up in conversation, you gladly confirm your fatalism. What happens must happen. The proof comes in that it happens. And for you, it was finished then. He was going to end you. You hadn't seen him. You didn't know who he was. You didn't know why he was going to kill you. No demands had been made yet. The carnage had just started—even if it had been going on for two thousand years.
   Now was it your turn,

             in the serenity of that sudden timelessness
within that tiny infinity—
                              eternity's antechamber?

There was no speeded-up film of your life. No thoughts for your loved ones. No breakdown or sobbing. A great calm. Above all the hope that it would not hurt, that it would happen fast.

Play dead I thought then fuck the pain he knows I'm not dead he's standing right over me he's going to finish me off with a bullet to the head so there it's over it will be quick too quick hope that it won't hurt that it happens fast.

Adrenaline. Oozing sweat. Delight. Elation. *BANG!* Omnipotence. Vengeance. *BANG!* Iblis walked down the steps heading to the floor. *BANG!* to the right. Ahead, bodies tangled together, wailing, moaning, cowering. To his left, the mixing board, flipped over behind metal barricade. *BANG!* The guy at his feet made a nasty jolt. Too funny. He was going to finish him off, with a bullet to the back of the neck, clean shot, when, all of a sudden, the house lights went up. So Iblis went into automatic firing mode, raised his weapon, and sprayed bullets on the panic, the shock, and the HOWLS.

The bullet did not come. The end did not come. You understood that it would not come, at least not right away, while the shell casings discharging from Iblis's weapon fell like rain on your face, neck, and back. Burning hot. He would not finish you off. Had he only seen you? One prostrate body among others—corpses, carcasses, everywhere, spread out, broken up, piled up.

You were alive. The pain was tearing you to pieces but you could move your legs. You were not paralyzed. That observation took over all others. Wounded, but not paralyzed. You felt relieved. Relief—that's absurd. It's not so bad, you thought, I am not paralyzed. Someone behind you was holding onto your calves. You had to play dead. You were alive. You were losing blood, and a lukewarm pool was forming under your thigh. Had to play dead. You felt the casings around you. You thought: souvenirs. You thought: evidence. You picked up two or three and put them in your pocket. They were very long. You wondered what the projectile that had torn through your body must have looked like if the casings were so enormous. I have looked it up: the cartridge measures about 2.2 inches, the casing itself 1.18 inches, and the bullet head (that bit of pointed metal that ripped your flesh apart) measured a little more than three-quarters of an inch, with an exact diameter of 0.30 inches or 76.2 mm.

You thought: have to survive. You had to play dead. Motionless. A pebble. Survive. You thought: alive. You thought: lucky. You thought: not paralyzed. You would have liked the fist that was holding your ankles to loosen its grasp some. It tightened each time you tried to relax your muscles. Had to play dead. Motionless like a pebble. To survive. Like Sigolène. I am a pebble. I am Sigolène. I am a pebble. I am Sigolène.

10

SIGOLÈNE WOULD BE IN YOUR TOP 10 of the people you love most in the world, if you were required to make such a list. You loved her the moment you saw her, the moment she smiled at you, the moment her sweetness wrapped around you. You hold onto your friendship like a barnacle holds onto its rock.[3] She weathered a trial much more traumatic than yours because she was at the headquarters of *Charlie Hebdo* on January 7, 2015.

For weeks, for months, you found yourself in front of her in a state of chronic distress, wanting to console her, comfort and support her, to give her your love, knowing that it was useless. You would forever stay on the surface of her despair, like those lotions for dry skin that tell us, in fine print, that they only moisten the skin's outer layers. Because you were outside of her tragedy. No matter the disaster, that border will never disappear. That solipsistic border creates, or reveals, all intimate calamity. Extreme suffering throws us back into our irreducible solitude, into our undeniable individuality. You do what you can to stay connected.

---

[3] Are you absolutely sure you couldn't have found something better?

As soon as you understood that those blasts came from firearms, you thought about Sigo. Unclearly. About others too. It wasn't intentional. Sigolène; that name, those three syllables, those images of her and all that is tied to her in your mind have scarred your brain. Your obsession was to play dead. Despite the pain. Despite the uncomfortable position. Despite the SHRIEKS, the shots, the chaos, and the blood flowing from your wound. Sigolène. Who survived. Who wrote that so poetic novel, *Le Caillou,* "The Pebble." What could be more motionless and immobile than a pebble? "I am Sigolène. I am a pebble."

The sentence took shape. It started to take you over, in a loop. You focused on it. A litany. A mantra. I am Sigolène. I am a pebble. Shots, screams, the sounds of impacts, of falls, of flight. Hell? I am Sigolène. I am a pebble. Everything grew both clearer and quieter. Crystal and cotton wool. Gunfire and the attackers' orders. You carefully took off your glasses and held them in your hand. An awkward reflex. I am Sigolène. I am a pebble. "Tell President Hollande that we have come to avenge our murdered brothers in Syria!" I am Sigolène. I am a pebble. The ringing of cell phones, almost always followed by a blast. "Shut up!" "Don't move!" Followed by blasts. I am Sigolène. I am a pebble. I am Sigolène. I am a pebble. You couldn't feel the pain anymore. You were there without being there. You couldn't see anything anyway.

I am Sigolène. I am a pebble.

In the space cordoned off by the barricade, on the other side of where you were curled up, half-Sigolène, half-pebble, you noticed movement. Whispers. You could not move. Gunshots, screams, SHRIEKS. You were powerless. You could only wait. You were going to get out of this because you were Sigolène. They thought you were dead because you were a pebble. Behind you, somebody was holding onto your ankles and calves, just above your boots. You instinctively felt it like a gesture of desperate brotherhood. That person was holding onto you. To life. Still the gunfire, and a sudden explosion. Something fell on your head, like dust—plaster, you thought. Then something else, a little warm—a piece of brain, you thought. The attackers were having fun throwing grenades from the upstairs balcony. Here's exactly what you were thinking: They were *having fun* throwing grenades. And they had decided to exterminate you, right there, in that concert hall they controlled. They were going to whack every last one of you, one by one. No one could stop them. You were almost serene. Fatalistic.

I am Sigolène. I am a pebble.

Neither a pebble nor Sigolène is mortal. You could do nothing but wait. Soon there was silence, only broken by increasingly distant blasts. An inhuman silence that you had never experienced before.

I am Sigolène. I am a pebble.

You were floating. You were in no pain, had no fear. Tranquilized. Beyond lucidity. Lying there on the Bataclan's sticky, blood-covered floor, your head in the shell casings, unable to get up, most likely soon to die but light, calm, Sigolène, pebble.

11

"TELL FRANÇOIS HOLLANDE that this is to avenge our fallen brothers in Syria!" Terrorists. Okay, we were all going to die. The guy didn't have any accent. I was ashamed to notice it.

I am Sigolène. I am a pebble. I had two rounds in my butt, or in my upper thighs. I didn't know if they had exited my body. I wasn't asking those kind of questions. I was not paralyzed. That's all that mattered. I was bleeding. I could not move. Behind you, somebody was holding onto your ankles. I was the stick that he or she was clamping down on to stop from shrieking. I could hear war around me. I was floating, both there and absent. Sigolène and pebble.

"Tell François Hollande that this is to avenge our fallen brothers in Syria!" That was absurd. I hadn't even voted for him.

Sykes-Picot. Sounds like a doubles team at Wimbledon. Daesh, Isis, Al Qaeda—we know they're the bad guys. Islam—we more or less get that. Sunni, Shiite—now things get complicated. The Middle East—nobody understands anything about that. The Near East—nobody can find it. Nevertheless, we can find nice people over there. Sure we can! In the desert, where they organized the World Cup, where they built a hotel in the shape of a sail. Nice people we do business with. It's good for growth and international trade. You wouldn't understand. Luckily, we've got specialists, serious people, not like those who would go to listen to Eagles of Death Metal.

Darling, no talking about business at the dinner table.

"Tell François Hollande that this is to avenge our fallen brothers in Syria!"

It was definitely Efrit who spit that out. He, and you, should have known that firing assault weapons on defenseless spectators, on the wounded lying on the floor, wouldn't stop air strikes on Islamic State bases. What's more, did you really know who was fighting who in Syria, Iblis? Your indiscriminate slaughter would not have saved one kid, one mother, one soldier. I would not have been teaching anything new. You were enjoying your day of glory. Raising a bloody middle finger. What would your father think? He's aloof. Or you didn't even have a father. Humiliated at the factory. Ridiculed by half-baked Frog comics on the airwaves. What? Well, if you can't take a joke. The best towel-head is a dead towel-head. Your father was from Normandy, and your mother was Algerian. The best towel-head is a cheese-head. That's less funny. You were avenging no one. You were incapable of locating Lebanon on a map. You were lost. You felt rage, but against nothing, against no one, because your enemy was invisible, your tormentors imperceptible. You were too dark-skinned to be here, too Westernized for over there. You would have liked to have envisioned a future, but you didn't believe in that anymore. They had lied to you too much. Liberty and fraternity shattered at the cloven feet of every man for himself. You didn't believe in the future anymore whereas, like all of us, you needed to believe. You needed values.

Efrit had told you about the projects. Bros that deal, sistas that excite. You were not like them, but you got them. You were not like them, but you were all alone. So you chose yourself a struggle, brothers, and a cause. It must not have been such a bad cause, because there were many of you who must feel abandoned, given the number of converted Europeans you ran into in Raqqa. Mommy's boys and small-time crooks, psychos and couples. Most of them more Islamist than the Prophet himself. Even if some of them got scared and tried to escape when things really started to heat up with the Kurds and the Free Syrian Army. You caught them and executed them. You didn't know anything about the Kurds' story, just that they were the enemy and that they fought really well. Attackers and victims living in the same world, that we can't bother to decode (much less improve). Who reads *Le Monde diplomatique* cover to cover? What gets better ratings, public radio or MTV? Nobody anywhere is trying to understand. Why vote when they are all rotten? It's easier to look scornfully at each other, and to fire into the crowd.

For ten points: What is the capital of Jordan?

Dictators set up on ramparts to protect our houses in the shock of civilizations. At least they are secular. Saddam wasn't such a bad guy, after all. And say what you want, but in Gaddafi's day we had peace.

And now for our bonus question! How many UN resolutions has Israel violated?

Democracy? They aren't ready for it. They didn't have the Enlightenment. Here's the proof: just look at how their famous Arab Spring ended … But wasn't that little guide who showed us around the Valley of Kings a sweetheart?

And don't forget, you can play our big game by texting "1" or "2" from your cell phones. Sabra and Shatila were (1) an Italian disco duo from the '70s, or (2) Palestinian refugee camps where the Lebanese Phalange murdered hundreds of civilians?

And the Black September Organization was maybe made up of altar boys?

Oh no! You are not going to start talking about politics again…

"Tell François Hollande that this is to avenge our fallen brothers in Syria!" Syria, Iblis, Syria! Had you ever heard about Mesopotamia? Where writing was born. The cradle of one of humanity's most beautiful civilizations: the Sumerian–Akkadians. What would you have had to say about the Achaemenid Empire or the Umayyad Caliphate? About those weapons dealers who have every interest to keep bombs falling and bullets flying (in France, the most well-known of them is a senator, a mayor, and a press magnate)? About the Hittites and the Hashemites? By firing on spectators in a concert hall, or on people seated on a café or restaurant patio, do you really think that you are honoring God, who is nothing other (and this is already a lot) than transcendent humanity? That you were settling injustice?

You were angry. You can't do what you did without being a little angry. And, it's horrible to admit it, without being brave. All of us most likely have that kind of drive—to defend our values, our loved ones, our friends, and our children, of course. Absolutely no need to have to feel what we would be able to do for them. Everything. Anything. Even the most craven of us is capable of great deeds if what is most sacred is damaged. Can't all that is sacred get along? Without lines of defense between "them" and "us," between those who worship and those who defile? For some, the mere fact that others do not worship, or not the way you should, is equal to desecration. Good Lord, to take up an assault weapon and fire on a crowd, to wipe out men and women lying on the floor, you do need some anger! And despair. And sadism? Where do these emotions come from? From a collapse of reason? From our collective failure to hold up the efforts of civilization? I am angry, too. With a polite, civilized anger. A bourgeois anger? An anger that takes the shape of novels, but nobody gives a damn about that kind of anger. It gets recycled and sweetened up by the market society. It becomes charming. A child throwing a tantrum, dope laid out on all the shelves, smiles in literary salons.

Anger. Bravery. Struggles to wage. Against those who oppress and disempower. Who dehumanize. Is it imperative to do it with weapons in your hands, or can we hope to win by setting an example, sowing the seeds, sharing? How can you topple those who divide, who spread famine, who speculate on the market? Those are the ones to attack, Iblis. Those who make us fight among each other. Attack ignorance and those who keep us ignorant. Attack screens. The spirit of competition and competitiveness. The golden calf. Attack traffic circles, and business developments, and pesticides. Attack selfishness and stinginess. Attack child molesters and drivers who turn without signaling. Help us discover Ibn Khaldun, the Emir Abdelkader, and Oum Khalthoum. Because there, by shooting human beings on the ground, shooting them in the back, you did not avenge your fallen brothers in Syria. You served the schemes of those who gain from the tension between communities in Europe. Always seek out who profits from a crime, who is hiding behind Lee Harvey Oswald and Jack Ruby. If not, then for the decision-makers in every corner, for those who fuel the monster-making factories in our cities, you are just a risk to take, a margin of error, collateral damage. A pawn who takes the life of other pawns, while the kings and queens on each side of the chessboard sleep soundly in the shelter of their towers.

"Tell François Hollande that this is to avenge our fallen brothers in Syria!" I had never heard anything more tragic.

As Seen from Outside: V

5/5/2016, 6:56 PM
Erwan.
   Fuck, Erwan.
   How do you expect me to write about that night?
How do you expect me to write about that night
without censoring myself?
   I didn't tell everything, even to you.
   About what shot through me.
   I can't.

5/5/2016, 7:01 PM
I am not going to tell you how I lived through that
night when I knew you were over there. What I've
already confided in you is yours alone. The rest
belongs to me. The facts and sequence of events are
of no interest.
   I found you on November 13. It's weird, right? So
many people lost loved ones in that chilling shitstorm.
And I found one. Before, you were at a distance,
a passing encounter, a fantasized acquaintance,
an intangible face sliding between two thoughts
and slipping away, chased off by other thoughts,
always, inescapably. And then, all of a sudden, you
were part of every second. That lasted hours. Hours
made of seconds packed with you inside. And anger,
tenderness, and fear.

A close relationship goes deep from thinking so hard about somebody, speaking to them at a distance, praying without believing, wishing like a kid, so hard your eyelids could crack ... That burrows out a nest in your heart. Of course. You can't deny those kinds of seconds.

Only those were one-way seconds. You can't know that, as I can't know your own horrible seconds. That night, you became someone close to me. I stayed far away, and even if that gap has been somewhat breached, I feel it will remain.

That's not a serious problem, you know.

It's something good, too.

We got rid of that absurd illusion that we can love each other "just as much" or "in the same way." That we can feel the same thing.

So we can love each other as we are, when we can, by opposing an undemanding sweetness against terror.

TRANSCRIPT OF VOICEMAIL RECORDED 5/5/2016 AT 8:18 PM

You piss me off, Erwan.

What are you getting at? What are you looking for?

What do you want us to say?

That we love you? We love you.

(chuckles)

You are pissing me off, because ... Those thousands of links created in my brain that night, those synaptic connections, those strong neural channels, overloaded, massive—how can you be measured faced with ... You can't. Anyway. All those connections were finally starting to get honed down, less powerful, when, *bam!*, three words from you and you make them a little bit stronger again, because you asked me to go back to that night, to retrace those tracks, to reactive them ... And once again, there you are, in me, next to me, like a second skin. It's hard to live with that. Someone at a distance who has become close. I don't know how to do it. I am still looking for how to do it. Because, you know, there's the rest, the rest of my life that hasn't moved an inch. How do you get close to somebody? Not somebody you grew up with or who little by little worked his way into your heart. Someone who wasn't there and then, *bam!*, thrown into the center, into the bubble of the nearest and dearest.

I don't know. I don't know.

5/6/2017, 10:14 PM

Hey.

Don't expect pathos. Don't expect pity. Don't expect anything sappy. Don't expect anything polished. Don't expect anything like that from me.

Because we found ourselves faced with crude violence, what I feel for you is violent. Of a killer softness. Unfathomably absolute.

...

To hold you in my arms. Hold you fucking hard. An absolute necessity, born that night, that has never really waned.

5/6/2016, 10:51 PM

I am going back over our messages. Those thousands of lines sent since November 13. And then the lines before that. Those few exchanges that went before the flood. Because there were a few. Pathways concerning you had already existed in my brain. Here's the proof: I dreamed of you. On November 10. On November 11. On November 12. I dreamed of you. How do you explain that, huh? Why just like that, just before?

5/6/2016, 11:43 PM

Do I try to inject some meaning into something that doesn't have any?

5/10/2016, 4:50 PM

"For the brain, what we think strongly feels as if we had experienced it."

A sophrologist threw that at me two days ago. I'll spare you the details of how I found myself talking to a relaxation therapist. A chance encounter. That sentence has been spinning in my head ever since. I immediately thought about you. About what I had lived through, in my mind, with you on November 13 and afterward. There were brief shared moments. My visit to the hospital, and those short, weightless hours stolen from our lives. But the rest is just hundreds of fragments projected by my imagination.

What we think strongly feels like something we have experienced …

In a way, that's true. Those fragments belong to my memories. I am able to drum them up just like memories when your skin was touching mine. I know your true caress and your dream caress. I know the look in your eyes, even when your eyes did not look at me.

Strange.

And so distinct.

For example, in the creases of my mind, I hold onto my own version of what you went through at the Bataclan. And in that version, I was there. Because, you know, I could have been there. I had seen that fucking Facebook post announcing your presence at the concert, and I told myself, why not? Looked like fun. So, if I had not had to work that night, I would have gone. I would have surprised you. And of course, right when I turned on my cell phone, right when I knew, it was your face that sprang up, and Version B was imposed on me. The one where I lived through that hell with you, the one where I held your hand while closing my eyes with all my might, the one where I played dead to avoid taking another bullet, the one where, lying on the Bataclan's sticky floor, I imagined myself somewhere else.

What we think strongly feels like something we have experienced.

Yes, that night, I imagined myself there with you, imagining myself somewhere else.

A terrifying look into the abyss.

Oh, I don't claim to have experienced what you did. My case is not psychiatric. Only literary. It was my version. As if projecting myself there could have rescued you. As if my imagination had the power to create a quiet bubble around you in the midst of the racket.

And maybe that worked. Maybe we were all there, all those who were thinking of you.

That might seem absurd, and yet, if my rational ego rejects this kind of childish belief, my emotional ego wants to give over to it.

Because it's beautiful.

And what is beautiful should be true.

5/10/2016, 5:40 PM
Stopping myself at that half-truth would be a lie.

On November 13, I did actually project myself over there. But I also imagined all that I wanted to live with you. The scope of possibilities. Fragile flames in the darkness of futures. That night, I lived whole lives in which you played a part. Different lives. Different parts. And I lived whole lives in which you were dead. You don't become a writer by chance, right ... As the characters in my novels keep following their paths in me well after I have finished writing, those dreamed-up lives ripple between my projects. I can do nothing to change it. You, the idea of you, has seeped into my future. And you—Erwan—are free to nestle there.

It's crazy.

Out of fear of losing them, of being disappointed, rejected, I put most of the people I know into the vast zone between far-off acquaintances and friends. You have no idea to what point I let so few people get close to my center. The potential intimate clashes that you represent frighten me and compel me to keep you at a distance. Don't let me do it. Or at least, not all the time. Okay? Because your ever-so-close presence is devastatingly meaningful.

...

Shit, I said there would be no pathos.
Too late.

...

Take care of yourself, Erwan. And take care of this nest that you have hollowed out in me. I know, I know.

You are not in principle responsible for what goes on inside my head. You have asked for nothing of all that I have lived through "with" you … Except, that's wrong. You are partly responsible. From the first look, the first words, up to what we shared after that. You crafted this tie that binds us and that November 13 strengthened at least as much as I did. Because you created it, remember. You came to me. And on that day, when nothing had happened but a smile, you are the one who slid me into your possible futures. You are the one who set himself to hacking my unconscious so that I would not be able to get you out of my head.

You were even the one who friended me on Facebook.

That shows your level of responsibility.

(chuckles)

So long, Pirate.

12

YOU HAVE THE SOUL OF A HERO. Which is perhaps
explained by your sign.[4] You have already saved the
world dozens of times, ended aggressions, caused robbers
to flee (not bank robbers; you'd let them be), and put
down evildoers. And at the end, a beautiful princess,
grateful and admiring, falls into your arms.

I had already imagined such plots around the age of
seven, saving Adeline Casse from hideous perils. You had
written what was most likely your first novel at that time.
Your brother and you still slept in bunk beds, with you
on top. Braving all danger, you saved Adeline from being
devoured by crocodiles. No crocodile had ever been seen
at Ballans,[5] but the imagination there ran wild. Between
dark, dank wine cellars, hay mows, grape-picking and
the harvest, woods and woodlands (the hazelnut trees,
aside from foodstuffs, supplied you with flexible wood
to make bows). Or at the foot of the huge cedar of
Lebanon offered by the botanist Bernard de Jussieu to

---

[4] "A man born under the sign of Leo is an idealist dreamer. If he were a character
in a fairy tale, he would certainly be a proud knight in shining armor, protecting
widows and orphans." *Elle.fr.*

[5] Where, nevertheless, Richard the First defeated his father Henry the Second on
July 4, 1189, thus becoming King of England.

the lord of the lands in 1734. You have hardly ever gone back. Your childhood home is deserted, Madame Fradin's grocery store has disappeared, but the school where Madame Bélis taught all the village children, in a single classroom divided into five grades, is still running. Serving the greater area now. Across from it is the square in front of Saint Jacques's church (Romanesque, renovated in the fifteenth century), with its monument to the war dead and its pitch for *pétanque*. And the low wall on which, one summer afternoon of your tenth year, the day before your family moved to the Gard, you kissed Christel, an older girl from Neuvicq-le-Château. You have kept the two or three letters she wrote you afterward, before she got bored of you. Can a hero be sentimental too?

On that November the 13, 2015, fate gave you the opportunity to truly show your mettle, full bore, on a stage gigantic enough for your inner superhero. However, as soon as you heard the sound of firecrackers, you obeyed the "Get down!" that followed. A hero does not obey. If he acts like everybody else faced with adversity, he would save no one. What's worse: you never got up to measure the gravity of the situation, then react with efficiency and self-control. You stayed cuddled up like a wuss against your metal barricade. To add injury to insult, a bullet penetrates your *butt* after five minutes.

A hero would have risen above that ludicrous situation and, despite the pain, would have pulled himself together to "send those bastards to hell" (in a husky voice, pain kept in check). Super Wuss cowered in his and his neighbors' blood, could not move, and feigned death. Super Wuss hid no one, protected no one, helped no one escape. Super Wuss dressed no injury, stopped no bleeding, cauterized no wound. Super Wuss was not used to the horrifying racket of assault weapons.

Not used to the HORRIFYING RACKET of a Kalashnikov's burst of gunfire.

War. At home. No images on the screen. Nothing that your brain could reconstitute between the lines of *Blood Dark*, or *Voyage to the End of Night*, or *The Kindly Ones*. No fleeting compassion, felt between a smoke and a phone call, after having heard on the radio that the battle rages on here or there. Within our democratic republic, within our cotton wool of privilege: barbary, fear, and shrieks.

SHRIEKS.

Not stylized. No Tarantino effects.

The blood was really sticky.

Death really had a smell.

Blasts not in Dolby Surround Sound® ripped future projects and well-wishing to shreds.

Fear. Powerlessness. Lying down with your own blood, that was truly sticky, that truly stunk. And the pain … On the big screen, your body can take one, two, three bullets and you keep on fighting, saving women and children first, under machine gun fire you fly a chopper, make yourself a tourniquet and grit your teeth before terminating the bad guys. On the big screen, the bullets don't hurt that much. In life, a 7.62 mm projectile, shot at point-blank range, even in the butt, makes you bellow with pain. (You BELLOWED—a sound you didn't think you were capable of producing, an unheard-of sound.) When a bullet penetrates the butt (you can't even imagine the leg or the chest) of a hero or a coward, he doesn't get up to save everybody, like he does on the screen, where things are so "real" that you can't tell the difference between true and false. Because it's realistic. It's real. Docu-fiction. TV reality. Inspired by a true story. We are no longer taught how to tell the difference. We don't teach languages anymore. Everybody has their avatar, their online profile. So we think everything's permitted. You, the silent, passive majority in France from 1940 to 1945, you feel it in your blood and bones.

In the middle of the chaos, the SHRIEKS, the blood, the panic, you missed out on the most beautiful opportunity of your life to become a hero. Your ego will most likely brew up an eternal bitterness because of it. If you had not been hit, would you have intervened? Would you have tried to flee? You get the feeling that you would have played dead. And you are ashamed of that. Your arrogance would dare hope that if you had not been alone, you would have tried to protect the person or people who came with you. Some did so that night—used their bodies to shield others. Heaven exists. That's for sure. You can't believe that such an extreme selflessness would go without reward. Heaven exists, and you are in it. You have saved the one you loved, a friend or a stranger. You are the pride of all humanity. Your names must never be forgotten. You. You threw yourself to the floor and played dead.

You are not a hero.

Even during those few minutes before being wounded, you did not think about standing up against them. Super Wuss. You have to live with that from now on.

To help you, out of the mud of your memory rises some not-yet-too-dilapidated fragments that, when put together, reveal if not a redemption, then at least a welcome balm. In fact, when the terrorists were pinned down backstage, you could twist your neck and make out the forces of order deployed around the bar. You wanted them to come and get you, of course, but not before the others. Not just you. You felt part of a whole. You wanted them to come and save everybody. Suffering, waiting, and hope were collective. You were a member of a great, wailing body. Really, it's not a literary turn. Not that your fate or your (physical) salvation was of no importance, but they were mixed up and linked with that of the other victims. Your fellows in pain. Your brothers in misery and fear. Save us all, or save no one. Because we all almost bought it there.

As Seen from Outside: VI

Friday, November 13, 9:30 am. Chassol invited me to catch some Martinique rays at his Big Sun concert (at Enghien-les-Bains, this time).

Thursday, the evening before, I told myself, *Okay, Becquin. You're gonna get off your ass this weekend and get some fresh air*. I had seen you had shared that you were going to the concert on social media. I didn't see anyone step up to go with you. All the same, what an idea ... Heavy metal. I could have surely gone and seen you shatter your spine, bouncing left and right, up and down. And yeah, with your hair, I would have got the whole picture. So why not? Why not go with you? But Chassol got in touch so early in the morning that he won the bet (the bet, you know, in Enghien, with its casino ... anyway).

Worried messages ran riot on my phone without me hearing them. I discovered them in front of the auditorium exit, smoking a cigarette with my friends. Of course, the news didn't come in the right order: Saint Denis, Bataclan ...

Bataclan ... Erwan

Erwan

Erwan

Erwan

Erwan

Erwan

Neurons ringing in alarm.

The first bullshit to cross my mind was to call you. Just like the fat fuckhead I am.

Allahu akbar. Thank God you didn't have your phone on you. Jeanne picked up, frantic.

Back in Paris, my buddy Mohammed and I stopped in a seedy restaurant in the Jaurès neighborhood. I ordered fries and some gluten-free thing. I don't know if I ate them (but I did drink a white Martini; necessary). I became like Jeanne. Frantic. Zoned out. With a huge desire to cry, but I mastered that fucked-up feeling. Not even in your dreams. He'll be fine.

I wanted to meet up with somebody, anybody, just not go home. It was already midnight, one in the morning. And because I'm not a teenager, I couldn't find anywhere to crash so late at night.

It was back home on my couch in the northern suburbs that I changed. I put myself in combat mode. Seated in my suit, TV on the news channel, computer on my lap, cell phone and bud in my right ear, landline in my left hand. Here we go. Emergency number dialed.

Acting without thinking is in my genes. Even a bull must think more than me before it charges.

Busy, busy, busy, busy, busy, busy, busy, busy, busy, busy, busy. I hit "redial," nervously, nonstop.

It was ringing!

That's when my brain started working again, and my heart started beating hard in my chest. Golgolita hadn't thought about what she would do if the news wasn't good.

Nobody picked up. The line went dead. Relief.

I took a deep gulp of oxygen and started again.

They ended up picking up. I ended up finding the words to ask the question. Ask if they had news about Erwan Larher. "I don't know any more where the 'h' goes."

They answered, with a petrified voice, "His name is not on the list for the moment."

For the moment.

The list of the dead. Erwan is not, for the moment, dead.

So, officially not, because his name is not written on the list.

I took a deep gulp of oxygen and started again.

Hospitals. I called all the hospitals in Paris. And ladies all told me the same thing: "Not here for the moment ..." And then they took my number to call me during the night if they had any news.

My brain started working again, and I started hating myself. What would happen if I fell asleep and was woken up by all the hospitals, one after the other? If I fell asleep and one of the ladies called me to tell me something? Something I would have had to repeat to Jeanne and Bertrand.

Anyway, I couldn't see how I could possibly fall asleep.

Everybody was looking for somebody on social media. Except those who went to sleep. It was 4 am at any rate. Not everybody had the job of taking care of heavy-metal-loving friends. Oh, it wasn't heavy metal? Okay, okay. I don't give a rat's ass. The singer was a radioactive shit pile.

And suddenly, the news came, out of nowhere, on another social media network, from a stranger. From a number that's missing two digits, from a hospital I didn't know, outside of Paris. Weird.

There was a kind of strange moment. Nobody reacted in that one second that seemed to last forever. I found the whole number and called.

After a few telephone problems, they connected me with the people working in the intensive care unit.

Intensive care.

I know what intensive care means. You leave with a toe tag, or you are not well for a very long time. You're not whole. They were going to connect me with someone. I was supposed to call Jeanne and Bertrand to tell them something ...

I wanted to throw the telephone through the window.

You know the rest. The guy was fine ... I repeated your name all night long. Like a crazy lady. I was right. You stayed with us.

We were traumatized but, physically, fine.

13

I AM SIGOLÈNE. I am a pebble I am Sigolène I am a pebble I am Sigolène I am a pebble.

The media stated that Iblis Saala and Efrit attacked a little after 9:45 pm. That around 10 pm, a local police officer and a member of the SWAT team broke into the concert hall through the main entrance, bearing handguns. They fired on Iblis, who, at 10:07 pm, wounded, detonated his belt of explosives. You had thought that he and his sidekicks had thrown grenades from the balcony. No. Two police officers had just saved dozens of lives. Because following Iblis's dismemberment, Saala and Efrit took refuge in a hallway with the hostages. End of the carnage.

Twenty minutes. You can measure the time span between two events you remember: the arrival of the attackers and the explosive disintegration of Iblis.

Twenty minutes. If they had asked you—and the investigators did so when they questioned you—you would not have known how to estimate the time span. It was both slow and quick. In a dimension other than the one of stopwatches and second hands, one regulated from the inside by emotions and feelings, instinct and animal drive. In under twenty minutes, you can go to the gym. You can spend twenty minutes sweating on the rowing machine. In twenty minutes, you can go from Montparnasse to Abbesses on a motorcycle. Would those twenty minutes be the same as the time that passed on November 13, 2015, at the Bataclan, between 9:47 and 10:07 pm? Come on …

I am Sigolène. I am a pebble I am Sigolène I am a pebble I am Sigolène I am a pebble.

When you talk about your experience, you explain that you went into a kind of trance. According to your friend Marie, you may have experienced an episode of depersonalization. You looked it up on Internet. That could work (derealization as well). She told me she had also gone through that. When she was young. Every time that her father hit her. What a fucked-up world.

At this point in your tale, the people you are conversing with generally have no more words, or just an adjective mumbled while shaking their heads ("crazy" and "incredible" are the most common terms). They hang on your every word, eyes wide open. Be careful not to get a thrill out if it. I know you. It's not as if you ever hated being the center of attention.

"Stop interrupting me!"

"Go right ahead."

I am Sigolène. I am a pebble I am Sigolène I am a pebble I am Sigolène I am a pebble. Trance? Depersonalization? Derealization? The silence that had started to crackle got you out of this altered state. A horrifying, thick, sticky silence, then only pierced here and there by ringing or buzzing phones, which rendered it even thicker, defining its contours, granting it rhythm, being its grisly accomplishment. A silence like a shroud that shyly showed its seams, revealing its secret little by little. It was woven with bated breath, secret murmurs, lives on hold. Like a snorting monster, the silence faded away into sighs, whines, sobs, and wailing. Pain, suffering, affliction, and distress took on an abominable shape, materialized by polyphonic dissonance that struck and chilled the very essence of your humanity. You were the one who was sighing, whining, sobbing and wailing. At that moment, every man and every woman in the world whined in twisted unison that tragic dull chant that insults the gods at the same time that it calls out to them. That dares them to come down here, into the orchestra seats of the Bataclan or the ruins of Aleppo, in Borno or the slums of Rio.

Then the cries and insults rose in crescendo. "Come and get me!" "What the fuck are you waiting for?!" "He's dying in my arms over here!"

You swung your head around as much as your position would permit. You were still lying on your side, your face against the metal barricade. Despite your limited angle of vision, you saw, up above, positioned against the bar, kneeling, masked gunmen. One in particular, directly in your line of sight, with the hard look of a guy ready to take someone down. Your Bruce, your hero. We're saved, you thought.

We were fucking saved!

Total relaxation. You were no longer Sigolène. You were no longer a pebble. There was a progressive return to reality, to the hard floor, to the discomfort of your situation. You hurt. You were numb and stiff. Behind you, a fist was still pinning your legs to the ground, holding stronger as soon as you tried to move a little. Not a problem. We were saved.

In fact, this was the beginning of your trials.

14

EVER SINCE YOU STARTED YOUR PROJECT B, you had consulted many Internet documents to try to establish your personal timeline inside of the official one. You found out that:

- The first members of the BRI, or "Anti-Gang" police commando squad, entered the building around 10:30 pm.[6]
- At 11 pm, the men of the RAID tactical unit took position on the dance floor to cover the members of the BRI going upstairs.[7]
- "The first of the five telephone conversations [between the RAID negotiator and the attackers] took place at 11:27 pm, the rest following at 11:29 pm, 11:48 pm, 12:05 am, and 12:18 am."[8]
- "Overall, it seems that all of the victims wounded on the ground floor were evacuated by the forces of order, from the concert hall to the lobby, then from

---

[6] Caroline Michel, "Le récit minute par minute de l'assaut au Bataclan," *Tempsréel. nouvelobs.com*, November 22, 2015.

[7] Ibid.

[8] "Rapport fait au nom de la commission d'enquête relative aux moyens mis en œuvre par l'Etat pour lutter contre le terrorisme depuis le 7 janvier 2015—Tome 1," *assemblee-nationale.fr*, July 5, 2016, p. 59.

the lobby to the emergency care units, before the final assault was carried out [at 12:18 am]."⁹

Given this data, as you were shot at the beginning of the attack, and that you had heard many exchanges between the person serving as the intermediary for the attackers and the RAID negotiator, it is plausible to deduce that you had been Sigolène and a pebble between 9:50 pm and 10:45 pm or 11 pm. Then wounded, aware you were bleeding out and fading away for over one hour, until your evacuation with the last wounded to the Bataclan lobby around midnight.

After you sighted your motionless saviors, you raised your arm to them two or three times in the space of twenty-some minutes. Not to draw attention to yourself, but to indicate that the person clutching your calf, a guy to your right, somebody else on the other side of the barricade, and yourself, were alive. To signal a pocket of life there, breath that was slowing, forces fading away.

Bruce's look, cold and determined at first, that of a soldier ready to take somebody down, changed as the minutes went by. "Don't move, Bruce. Those are our orders!" Bruce obeyed. Powerlessness started to wear him down. Survivors cursed at him, victims were dying in the orchestra level before his eyes, eyes in which you can then make out despair.

⁹ Ibid., p. 60.

Bruce was still not moving. Orders. He was a soldier.

In his baby blues, pain and anger drowned out despair. His face can only show you what his mask allows. He looked young. It might have been his first time on the ground. He had never seen so many corpses in one place. Had never smelled such a stench. The dying wailed, the healthy insulted him, the wounded asked for his help. Bruce could not intervene. That was eating him up, but the orders were to wait until the scene was secured. So he was falling apart behind his mask and his bulletproof vest. Hindered brotherhood was thinning down the warrior.

In that reactivated time stretched out between hope and pain, you were growing weaker and more impatient. You were scared that your wound was serious. You were wondering why they weren't coming to get you. You were getting irritated. What are they fucking doing?! They were just there, four yards from you! Were their superiors afraid to send them into the fray of the dance floor, where the enemy could shoot at them from the balcony? The gunfire had stopped for a while. You couldn't see much. You couldn't move. You were dwindling away. You were full of anxiety. You were getting all worked up all by yourself in your own blood. You were cold.

During that listless time, it looked as if they were finally starting to evacuate the victims. You realized that the concert hall was all lit up, and that the metal barricade to your left was on the ground. You were growing numb, and you hurt.

You saw a man go by, pushed by a policeman but with a haughty gate, his torso naked, hands behind his back, a diabolical and victorious sneer on his face. You told yourself that they got one alive.

From then on, lots of commotion. Orders were shouted out. A voice cried out that they had hostages and gave a telephone number. Another voice had the number repeated. That would have been silly if you hadn't been in such pain. You raised your arm, but you couldn't keep it up.

In that time drawn out by suffering and impatience, a commanding voice rose up. "All right! Everybody who can get out, come toward us. Hurry, hurry, hurry!" Something like that. You don't know anymore. Motion, shouts, protests. "But we can't fucking move!" "And we are just supposed to die over here, is that it?!" The sound of stomping close by (you were laid out not far from the steps that led to the exit). You told yourself that you had to try, at least try, to crawl … Impossible. You were aware of how ridiculous you were. Nailed to the ground. You had to wait, again, pathetic, interminable pause. Had you just remained a pebble, stone, a husk, non-real?

It was long.

It was hard for you.

Suddenly there were two men over you. Looked like cops. Tense. Anxious. Each one grabbed you under an armpit. Harshly. You caught a glimpse of a young woman, seated against a pillar, head tilted to one side. You believed that she had a hole in her shoulder, but you were weak, could have been delirious. You tried to smile at her. You wondered if she was the one who had been grabbing onto your legs. Your saviors dragged you over the steps without the slightest concern for your health, then threw you against a metal barricade. They hurt you. They hurt you bad. They did not care, almost chewed you out for not being cooperative enough. They used their improvised stretcher to drop you off at the top of the lobby stairs. You stayed there a long time, next to other wounded, as a jumble of legs and hips brushed against you, stepped over you. An indifferent, busy, upright ballet.

A woman in dark clothes bent over toward you and quickly examined you. Clinical. Blank-faced. You believe that it was at that moment that your jeans were cut for the first time. You think that she told you she was a medical examiner. You think she put a tag on you. You barely had the time to say anything and she was already gone. You were in a bad way, stretched out on the cold metal. You seemed to understand that they were evacuating the wounded in order of priority. You had had it. You didn't say anything. You were alive. You were just a waiting body. Helpless. Powerless.

One hundred years later, people were finally bustling around you, then carrying you away on your godforsaken, ad hoc stretcher. The guys were having trouble in the steep staircase that led down to street level. The pain was indescribable. Your brain went into protection mode and sent you into a virtual haze.

The street.

Finally, fresh air ...

The cold.

Police vans.

Faces.

People on the phone.

Police officers.

You were saved.

A feeling that it was not real. Of being an extra in a film. Or the hero of your own biography. You wondered what you must look like, if you would look good on TV (you need more than a bullet in the nether regions to kill off narcissism, it would seem). We went across a street. You were cold. You hurt. We turned. You wobbled on the metal. You were shivering. You were saved. They were going to take care of your wounds.

At least that's what you thought then.

15

I DIDN'T THINK ABOUT ANYBODY.
Didn't draw courage from any love, any friendship. Didn't draw any courage. Didn't need any.

I didn't tell myself that I had to hold on for this or that reason. I didn't tell myself that I had to hold on. Or that I had to get out of this. I wasn't *holding onto life*.

I suffered through.

I didn't pray. I didn't promise myself to become a better person if I got out of this. I didn't sob. I wasn't pitying myself or bemoaning my plight.

I was waiting.

I didn't ask myself if people on the outside were worrying about me. I wasn't thinking about the outside. Not at all. I was completely floor sticky with blood, completely hemorrhage, completely hands clutching my ankles, completely now, completely animal, completely bruised body against a metal barricade. Completely pebble, then completely waiting.

I only realized two days later that people were terrified for me. Whereas me, I was not at all terrified for them. Ever since, I have been ashamed of that.

I discovered all that love. It changed the bullet's trajectory. Don't try to convince me otherwise.

As Seen from Outside: VII

The evening of the 13th, I was at a weird party, at a loft where I knew almost nobody, near the Château d'Eau Métro. I was thinking about how to slip away unnoticed when a rumor started to make the rounds. *They say there has been an attack in the neighborhood.* Then: *There are gunmen scattered all over Paris.*

... And then the news hit: *Hostages taken at the Bataclan.*

I found a quiet corner. I sent you a message. I don't remember anymore—wait, hold on, I'll find it: "Larher, Eagle of Metal, tell me you're okay."

And then, no answer.

In the loft, the word spread: Nobody move. We're here for the night. It was clearly obvious. Our first curfew. I was getting ready for that too. But when around 10 pm I heard a group near the bar talking very seriously about THE event of last week (a Balmain collection that had drawn a mob in front of H&M stores), I got the hell out of there.

I remember when I went out the door, it was seen as a kind of heroism. For the guests at that party, I was the guy who was breaking the curfew. At the time, I also experienced it a bit like that. For a very short amount of time. Because once on the street, in the real world, everything looked much less dangerous. Almost normal.

In the Métro, people who knew informed others, but not even all that much, I think. It was rather quiet. And it was only after two stations that I thought: "Fuck, Jeanne!"

I got off at Marcadet station. I walked fast. The party with the nutcases at Château d'Eau was already very, very far behind me.

Below Jeanne's building, I bought a bottle of Coke. A little voice in the back of my head told me, no alcohol. It also told me that this might be a long night.

It was only once I was upstairs at Jeanne's place that I understood the situation.

In a corner, your telephone and papers were on the floor.

It must have already been 11 pm. The France Info radio station had started to repeat its reports. Little was changing. We only knew that some people were able to escape the Bataclan. The rest was still in the works.

I remember that Jeanne's TV was broken, and we told ourselves that that was a stroke of luck. Because if it had been working, we couldn't have stopped ourselves from watching a news channel.

For the rest, I don't know too much anymore about what we talked about. The assault had begun. We were waiting for a phone call. We told ourselves that, at any rate, you would end up borrowing somebody else's telephone and calling your own number. Text messages came. We couldn't know who was writing. When the phone rang, Jeanne answered quickly that we didn't know.

The rest of my memories, of course, are in splinters.

I don't know any more what we talked about, but I don't think we talked much about you, and less and less. We must have been afraid to let a sentence in the past tense slip out. Twice, I'm pretty sure (I don't know if Jeanne felt the same way; we have never talked about it) we were about to hold each other in our arms, and then didn't. I told myself (it's weird how I am convinced that she told herself this too) that if we had, it would mean that we didn't have much left to believe in and might fall apart. And that was out of the question.

I've said it before, and I'll say it again: Jeanne was incredibly strong. And I just told myself that I had to be strong for her. But that was a little later in the evening. In the meantime, the radio had started broadcasting a toll-free number to get information. Jeanne called, once. No one picked up, and we didn't call it again. Or only once more. I was like her. I told myself that we weren't going to block the lines.

I also remember that I wanted to pee (Thanks, Coke!), but I couldn't. I spent two minutes in the toilet, and nothing came. I listened to Hollande, the journalists, the eyewitnesses on the radio, and then more breaking news hit. So I zipped up my fly and went to listen to it with Jeanne.

It was like that every fifteen minutes, with developing reports (less and less so), we reassessed the chances: the Bataclan's total capacity minus the number of dead reported minus the number of people who escaped at the beginning of the attack = Larher's chances.

For the rest, we made conjectures. We must have written quite a few scenarios in the emptiness.

And then the news started to loop. We turned the radio down low. We turned up the volume for breaking news, and we started calculating again.

The other big activity was Facebook, with the computer on the table. Before I got there, Jeanne had started to create a group with all those who were asking for news. I added names left and right from the pages of friends I saw. There once again, we didn't talk about it, Jeanne and I. And maybe I'm wrong here, I hope I am, but after 1 am I started to think that she was preparing that list of people she might need to contact at the moment *when*.

When.

But then once more, of course, we carefully avoided those words.

We only talked about the chances that remained. We hesitated to call the toll-free number, and then didn't.

Around 1:30 or 2 am, Charlotte called.

She had managed to get someone on the toll-free number.

He wasn't on the list of the dead!

Joy lasted one minute. It was intense, and then we looked at each other: *he doesn't have his ID with him*.

We kept adding people to the list—all the people writing on their wall that they were worried about Erwan Larher.

On the Facebook group page, Myriam posted the address of the Paris police commission page where you could notify them of disappeared persons. Jeanne filled out the form. I remember that that was a relief. We didn't hesitate anymore about calling the toll-free number. Trust in the departments of the State. They would call us back. We only had to wait.

So, while waiting, we held onto our most optimistic scenario. Our slightly crazy hope. You had been wounded, too serious to be able to give your name or a number, but just wounded. And you had been taken as an unidentified victim to a hospital.

The radio was off.

I don't have the slightest idea what Jeanne and I could have talked about. I think we started to compare the way we had experience the events—how all of this was different from the Charlie Hebdo events of January. In January, everything was just about togetherness. We drew up our memories of the march on January 11. By this time, I don't think we even commented on the various declarations on the radio. Those were just words. We only lived through this Event in an intimate manner. Everything coming from the outside only fed our calculations. Rational, rational. Evaluate. Analyze. That was reassuring. Rational to the point of being irrational, perhaps. But now I'm starting to be literary.

The other thing that was with us, if I may, was your mother.

We had talked about her when I got there. Jeanne had told me that your parents were in Vietnam. She had hesitated to call them. We told ourselves we shouldn't. There was most likely nothing worse than to call a mother more than sixty thousand miles away to tell her that we didn't know anything. And then, at any rate, Jeanne hadn't found her number in her old-fashioned telephone. We then just wisely set the question aside.

Except that, with waning hope, at 3 am, we told ourselves that, yes, we were going to look for the number again.

Jeanne had your phone in her hand when your mother called.

They would have already told you everything themselves. I just want to insist on one thing: I heard nothing on the other end of the line, and that was impressive. And Jeanne was incredible. Factual, relating information, in order. It was only in the following weeks that I became aware of the enormous amount of energy that that phone call must have drained from her. And that night as well.

Because, for me, a friend's life was at stake. I had just started to understand that we were living through this, through this kind of thing that we knew existed but that we never thought we'd have to live through. Anyway, I had started to understand that for me it was already huge, but for Jeanne it was so much more. It was an enormous part of her future that was at stake.

Maybe I shouldn't have written that.

Fine, I'm just saying that at that time, we didn't believe we were going to get any good news.

At any rate, I didn't.

You know the rest, pretty much.

Jeanne was exhausted, but it was out of the question to go to sleep in her bed. A little before 4 am, she took her duvet and rolled herself up in it in the living room, at the foot of the coffee table where the Coke bottle was almost empty and the ashtrays full.

I stayed seated on the couch, in slumber mode, on the watch for what would happen. It's crazy the place Facebook took that night. And what happened on the feed was pretty beautiful. Above all, what it showed: all those people who were on the move without our knowledge, while we were stuck in waiting mode on rue Damrémont.

It was just fifteen minutes later, on the feed, that Séverine shared the tweet she'd got from the guy at Mondor hospital.

I don't know what I said. I didn't shout, but damn near. Jeanne woke up with a start. But you already know the story. She didn't turn to me. She rushed to the door.

Those few minutes were a little nuts. We still didn't know anything, outside of the word "alive." We went back a little to the "No, we aren't going to block the lines" act. And then Charlotte's message came fast. She had managed to get the emergency room. I think that no one and nothing could have resisted Charlotte's verve that night.

A bullet in the butt. HE WAS FINE.

So, for the first time that night, Jeanne lost it. And it was beautiful. She started jumping all over the apartment and screaming, "He's fine! He has a bullet in his butt!" Because at that time, saying "butt" was a little bit like a kid saying "fart." It meant that it wasn't serious.

Jeanne was jumping all over the place. I must have jumped into her arms, but my memory of those fifteen minutes ... It's about my total inability to react, to break out of the cold demeanor.

... I said that, but it's wrong. I took a look a few days afterward at the messages that I must have sent, with all the typos and exclamation points of absolute relief. But if you were to ask me what I remember from those minutes, the answer would be me, like a damned idiot, standing next to the table where the computer lay, thinking, "Hey guy, are you going to react or something?"

As if I had gone through all the stages of grief in fast motion since 10 pm. (That's of course wrong, and fucking stupid, but that's how I explained it to myself.) The Announcement was like a second shock, a backlash of disbelief.

Anyway.

The next hour was spent sending messages all around, Jeanne on Facebook, me answering unknown numbers on your fucking phone, each message taking ten minutes, and getting somehow ready for the next day. I remember that Jeanne really wanted to go the hospital with Charlotte, and I thought, "I want to come, too!"—a stupid little thought that took me back to that Emmanuel Carrère book when he tells the story of how his girlfriend went to help the rescue workers after the tsunami, and how he stayed at the pool feeling like an idiot and a little jealous. This was, however, obvious: Charlotte would always be The One Who Spread the News. She was, quite frankly, life itself. That night it was a bit as if she had gone right to the Bataclan to get you out of there.

I could have gone home, but I didn't want to. I went to bed around 6 am on Jeanne's couch. I must have gone to sleep around 7:30 am. (Thanks, Coke. Thanks, Daesh.) At 8 am, the police commission woke us with a call to Jeanne to tell us you were alive.

And it was already the day after. I went to get croissants at the bakery. The street was almost deserted, and it felt weird to say such things as "Thanks," "How much do I owe you?," "Have a good day."

Then in the car, heading to Mondor through Bondy.

From his bed, Larher talked about his night with such precision and virtual detachment that we told ourselves while leaving that the backlash might be very painful. But all that was nothing compared to the thoughts that fueled us twelve hours earlier.

Two final memories from the car.

The first from the trip there, when we heard the words of Hollande—"acts of war." That was the first moment I really grasped the Event as a whole, and when we immediately understood that the aftermath was going to be ugly, very ugly.

The second memory, on the way back. A little voice inside of me was worried about this layer of coldness that stuck to my reactions. But when we got on the beltway, it took me four exits to realize that I had taken the wrong direction, south. I think that I could have taken the highway against the flow of traffic while continuing to tell myself, "It's kind of weird to act so normally after that."

The drive through Paris later did us well. I dropped off Jeanne, we talked about the party to come at Vincent's place where we were going to celebrate life a little, at any rate. I parked the car in the garage. I turned off the engine. And then, I started to weep. It was so good.

12:05 am. I notice that the default font for OpenOffice is called Liberation Serif.

Others would tell you about the following days.

I will always remember the exchanges that happened over the Facebook feed, about hospital visits and what we could all do. It was beautiful on many levels. (I am not just talking about reactions or comments from this or that person. There was something more than that. A spirit of togetherness that we all hooked into, with a mix of rushed enthusiasm and restraint.)

And then there you were at Mondor with that big teddy bear.

I wasn't expecting it, but then, *BAM!* A huge emptiness for a month. No desire, no future plans, nothing. All that energy that got stuffed into that night. And the whole week answering people who were asking for news. (I am repeating myself, but once again, Jeanne was incredible.) And then, a total allergy to high-minded words and to where they come from.

That was the first year that I truly loved Christmas with my family. It was only after that that I think I found my energy again.

Oh, and if you want an epilogue, I'd like to bring up one last moment.

It was that other night, coming back from the wine bar. You were joking about the night of November 13, and about what we were doing then. I said, "I was with your gal, buddy," and I almost didn't flinch before saying it. Jeanne laughed. That did me a world of good.

16

THE STREET.
    Finally, fresh air ...
The cold.
The police vans.
The faces.
People on the phone.
You were saved.

A feeling that it was not real. Of being an extra in a film. Or the hero of your own biography. You wondered what you must look like, if you would look good on TV at that very moment. We went across a street. You were cold. You hurt. We turned. You wobbled on the metal. You were shivering.

There was a kind of courtyard, totally dark. Your stretcher carriers slid you down from the barricade, still without the slightest delicacy. That fucking hurt, beyond pain. Other wounded people all around you, screams, whining, more commotion. You were growing weaker and weaker. You were letting go, lying on the ground, ink-black sky overhead, shivering, strength gone, bled out, frozen, unable to speak.

Resigned.

Next to you, it sounded like the noise of a defibrillator.

Whomp! Followed by *beeeeeep*! Characteristic of cardiac resuscitation. You were under the impression that the wounded person had perished. Your teeth were chattering. It was uncontrollable. A fireman stopped next to you. You don't know any more how it happened, what he asked you, if you answered him. You must have told him you were cold, because he left, then came back with a survival blanket. He kneeled next to you. He couldn't have been twenty-five. Blond, short hair. The first real human contact since the beginning of the nightmare. Your Angel. You felt his manic energy, but he showed nothing. He took your hand. "Hold on. You're going to make it. We're going to take care of you." You were stunned by the rescue workers who had dragged you here to leave you on the ground, and the absence of ambulances, of emergency vehicles. "There have been other events in Paris. There aren't enough of us," shouted one of the duo. You told the Angel that you hurt, asked for a painkiller. They had no medicine. Only the presence of this darling fireman stopped you from passing out, from fainting. You asked him, teeth still chattering, seized by pain, cold, and anguish, if you could lie your head on his lap. The position was not very comfortable for him, but he accepted. He held your hand tightly. "Stay with me. We're going to take care of you." You thanked him, mumbled that he was great. Tears were in his eyes. "Don't worry." You had been there for centuries. The survival blanket had zero effect. You wanted to leave gently, bled out and frozen, your head on the Angel's lap—who demanded that you hold on, promised you he had alerted the medical team about your presence, your situation. You didn't believe him. You didn't give a damn. You were almost not even there. It was gentle.

The dark sky, the cold, your Angel, the sudden proof that we are souls inside of bodies, a tranquil soul taking leave of your numb body, your useless body. And another bit of proof superimposed itself. One must never die alone, but holding someone else's hand.

A silhouette looked at the tag the doctor in the Bataclan lobby had stuck on you (on your wrist?). It looked as if someone had decided that it was time somebody took care of your case. They transported you on a real stretcher this time, what seemed (you don't remember any more) like a few steps away from the dark courtyard where you had been lying since the Dawn of Time. They set you down. Were they examining your wound? At any rate, there was light there. It was a fucking mess, too. In the middle of the moaning, everybody was calling out, hailing each other. A feeling of utter improvisation, of stress. They sometimes got irritated. Absolutely no coordination. You could recognize the doctors by their calm and certain gestures.

The Angel muddled through an apology. "I'm sorry. I've got to leave you. There are other wounded. I'm needed." His eyes were tearing up again. Yours too. He was apologizing for going to help other victims? You shook his hand. Hard.

"Of course! Go!" you sighed out. "Thank you. Thanks for everything."

You would like to see the Angel again. Buy him a drink. Probability that you would cry in your beer = 99%.

Once more, you waited.

Semi-conscious, you felt that someone was finally moving you. Evacuation? They placed you on a new stretcher. The pain, fuck, the PAIN! You squealed, too worn out to shriek. You were so weak. The stretcher reached a firefighters' van. The rescue worker, also very young, was in a complete panic. He was looking for his superior, who had to drive the van. After a perilous and painful transfer, you found yourself lying down in the back, on a metallic surface, up high. It wasn't a vehicle designed to transport the wounded. The stressed-out rescue worker did what he could to get you set up. There was nothing to attach you. Another victim was lying on the van floor.

"Stay there!" the kid screamed.

As if we were going to run off.

"Where the hell is What's His Name?" he howled while getting out of the van, before turning to us. "Stay calm, everything's fine, I'm going to get my superior! We can't leave without him!"

You weren't in any big rush. It must have been four hours since you had been shot. You couldn't see the person lying on the floor. You could hear his raspy, hoarse breathing. Just before being taken care of, you started to understand that the rescuers were mixing up the casualties, one seriously wounded with one less seriously, so as to not wind up with hospitals full of serious cases and others that would only treat lighter cases. You managed to get a glimpse of your (future) traveling companion. In fact, his situation looked much bleaker than yours.

After five, or two, or ten minutes of waiting, Stressed-Out Rescue Worker finally came back. He had found his superior. We could now go. They both got in front, leaving us alone in back.

"Hold on to something!" he shouted.

To what? There were no handles or edges. Nothing to grip or grasp. The driver took off, hit the sirens. And we were off on one of the most harrowing drives of your life. Up until then, the prize had gone to a Puy-Sainte-Répard to Aix-en-Provence commute when you were 19 years old.

17

FRED, JEAN-MI, BILL, AND YOURSELF, all students at the Institute for Political Studies at Aix-en-Provence, had been co-renting a house stuck between fields, vineyards, and woods on a wine-growing property since the beginning of the school year. You had all organized get-togethers, parties, concerts, dinners, and, from time to time, worked on your research project. That night, there were a dozen of you, ever so slightly tipsy. Around midnight, you got hungry. Nothing left to eat at the house. One of the participants, who you barely knew (it was common to wake up and find perfect strangers sleeping on the couch), told you he had a sandwich in the side door pocket of his car. You went outside. God knows why, but you were in your stocking feet. You got close to the Good Samaritan's convertible and bent over the car door. You stepped on something sharp. You found the (half-eaten) sandwich, went back to the house, and rejoined the little party.

After a few minutes, you became aware that your foot hurt. You wondered if you had not stepped on a villainous pebble, but on a dead wasp. Yes, that's stupid, but you were trashed. You paid hardly any attention to it and kept on partying.

Your leg started to hurt. You pulled up your pant leg. Your calf and ankle were swollen. You were struck with worry. You talked it over with your buddies. Their already blissful state had been amplified by the hysterical qualities of a sizeable amount of hashish straight from Amsterdam. Not keen on breaking the mood, you said that you could wait a little but a trip to the hospital might be on the agenda. Everyone thought your remark was hilarious. Given their state, if you had set yourself on fire in the middle of the living room, they would have found it hilarious.

You had another drink. You were no longer in the swing of things. You suddenly thought about a snake. Your leg was numb, almost limp, and all swollen. You took off your sock and looked at the bottom of your foot. There was a small red wound. You asked a friend to take a look down there. The marks supported the theory of a bite. Somebody stated there hadn't been any vipers around Aix for ages. Somebody else declared that vipers love hot weather and one could have very likely had a little nap on the exhaust pipe of the car. Jokes all around. You felt bad. You felt a pang in your heart. Little red tracks appeared on the sole of your foot.

All went into commotion. How many cars do we have? Who is in a fit state to drive? You got yourself ready in haste. You found yourself in the two-seater convertible sports car of the Good Samaritan. A car full of inebriated buddies led the way, made mostly of downhill hairpin turns. You started to fret: viper bite, sudden heart attack, dead man's curve … You saw the venom coursing through your veins right to your heart. Your driver didn't drive very well. He confessed having got his license the day before. On top of it all, he was hammered. You were pale, holding onto the car door. You were going to die, either poisoned or the victim of a car accident. As a teenager, you had always dreamed of having a rock 'n' roll smash hit. You were now going to end up rolling down rocks and getting hit and smashed. The Good and Drunk Samaritan scraped against the hillside, crossed the traffic lines, made the transmission squeal. The whole time driving down, and the expression works royally, a highway to hell. You were getting psychosomatic. You were sweating. Your leg seemed to both weigh a ton and no longer be part of your body.

By a miracle, you arrived unscathed at the emergency room, after having run two red lights, ignored countless rights of way, smashed into many curbs. Luckily it was late, and there wasn't a lot of traffic.

You went into the lobby. You froze up. Two police officers were visiting with the receptionist. Their heads slowly swiveled toward the six or eight drunken fools who had just broken onto the scene. Suspicious looks. Your friends played it cool. You went toward the counter.

"I've been bitten by a viper," you sputtered.

The girl looked at you as if your nose had been sticking out of your forehead.

"Calm down, sir. What's going on?"

"I'm telling you I was bit by a viper!"

Two or three chuckles were heard from those in the waiting area, seated on the chairs against the wall behind you. The cops grew stealthily closer. The receptionist raised her eyebrows.

"So, a viper, you say."

"Yes, a viper."

A moment passed. She glanced at the two police officers, who stared at you more than suspiciously.

"Fine," the receptionist remarked. "Show me your ID. We're going to fill out a …"

"I have been bitten by a viper! The poison has reached my heart! You have to call a doctor right now!"

You had leaned toward her. You had looked straight into her eyes. You had spoken with a firm voice through clenched teeth.

She picked up her telephone.

Then you were in your boxers, all hairy, stinking of alcohol, lying on a stretcher on wheels. Your right leg had tripled in volume. It was swollen, as if filled with water, and numb. The intern taking care of you was, by chance, stunning, wasn't wearing a bra under her lab coat, and smelled very good. Shame bogged you down. A very know-it-all redhead came to see you, declared forthright that there were no vipers left in the region. "Ha ha ha ha! Now let's see what you've got here, little joker!" He shot a wink at the intern. Fifteen minutes after examining you, he came back knowing fuck all. Frankly puzzled. "Well look at that. I've never run across such a thing. It's certainly a viper. We can see the fang marks. The symptoms match."

He left scratching his head. The sublime intern smiled kindly at you. She had most likely seen past your pathetic appearance and your laughable position. Flirting with her was tempting. You strived to get back a little dignity and dared two or three witticisms. You slipped in that you were a student at the Political Studies Institute. That didn't impress her at all. She explained to you that they didn't have any anti-venom, and that an ambulance was going to take you to Marseilles. "I'll be back," you said to her with a certain complicity, even a bit of intrigue. That's what soothed you in your trials. A beautiful story could come out of an absurd bite. It was destiny that put your foot in front of the viper's maw. A romance could well begin thanks to a few erotic ploys, right?

Your paramour returned, alas, accompanied now by the redheaded doctor and five or six other interns. Shame came back with a vengeance. Luckily you hadn't started the foreplay all alone. You had thus become the living subject and guinea pig of a lecture on vipers and venom, which sapped you of all your Casanova pretentions.

18

THERE WERE NO HANDLES OR EDGES. Nothing to grip or grasp. The driver took off, hit the sirens. And we were off for one of the most harrowing drives of your life.

From the first turn, you almost crashed onto your fellow traveler below. The stainless-steel surface you were lying on was slippery as hell. You just managed to catch yourself. You hurt. You were weak. Your trip in a spin-dryer set on hydraulic jacks lasted an eternity. Without ever slowing down, the daredevil drove on sidewalks, drove off of them, brutally changed directions, seemed to bank some corners on two wheels, to such a point that you were taken by fits of laughter. Even if the thought crossed your mind that you were going to die, not from a bullet at the Bataclan but in the cursed fireman's van that was supposed to save you. It was long. You were banged and knocked about. It was long. Not a single break. And the siren tearing through everything. It was long. You visualized the cars making way, moving to the side of the road. The drivers had to have imagined that this was linked to the *events*. It was long. You were wondering where you could possibly be going with such a long commute.

Paradoxically, you were in a pretty relaxed mood when, once the crazed vehicle had stopped, the back doors opened. You were two times a survivor.

They transferred you onto a stretcher. The pain, the fucking pain.

They pushed you past the glass doors.

You were saved.

And there you were all of a sudden, the hero of one of those hospital-based TV series that you could never stand to watch (sissy). The script was perfect, the casting impeccable. Everyone knew what to do. Everyone knew their lines.

"Gunshot wound?" a doctor, or a surgeon, asked you. Looked like a chef, both calm and rushed.

"Yes," you answered. "Shot twice."

BANG! BANG! You could still almost hear both blasts, almost simultaneous. You would learn the next day that you were only hit by one bullet. It was the double explosion of pain that was behind your mistake. The bullet entering, and then exiting. Little hands all around you made the world enchanting again. They took your pulse, took off your rings, examined you, put a wristband on you, reassured you.

"Do you want to hold onto your jeans?" the ER chief asked.

"I'd rather hold onto my ass."[10]

---

[10] I invite anyone to look me straight in the eye and tell me I didn't come up with that turn of phrase.

Snip! Snip! A few scissor cuts and that was the end of your favorite skinny jeans.

You can see yourself spread out on your stretcher, your pants in tatters, both legs open from top to bottom, in low-riding cowboy boots with socks showing, and slightly form-fitting boxers covered in blood. So you tried to be funny, even more so because among the caregivers busy at your bedside you could make out a charming face. Well, why not? You would have had it all. You had become a character from *Spinal Tap*.

There was commotion around the other stretchers too. You noticed haste tempered by professionalism in the voices of the medical workers. "OR, Stat." And, "I've got a transfusion here. Let's go." You trusted them. Their faces beamed with empathy despite the urgency and tension. Every look and every gesture told of a heartbreaking humanity and fraternity. You were really very weak. You had been losing blood for five hours. You were petrified. You were cold. You hurt. Your clothes were ripped up, sticky, but your brothers and sisters were taking care of you. Finally. Solidarity, altruism, and empathy lit up that room much more than the fluorescent bulbs did.

Shit! Everybody must have thought you were dead! You had to tell somebody that you were alive, immediately. You didn't know where your telephone was (at the coat check with your jacket? at Jeanne's place?). You had maintained a distant relationship with that object, sometimes forgetting to turn it on, sometimes forgetting it existed. You refused to acquire a recent model, whose usefulness would make no sense to you because you didn't want a cell phone connected to the Internet. You hated that postmodern fashion to be among beings through an interposed screen, between the permanent staging of the self and the day-to-day as selfie. Your old-school snobbery might have saved you. The attackers readily shot those unlucky people whose telephones started to ring. You borrowed a cell phone from an orderly within earshot of your poor, quivering voice and dialed the only number you knew by heart, because it was so easy to remember— Poopy's number. She didn't pick up. You left a message.

The charming face didn't ask you if you wanted to hold onto your boxers and bluntly cut them off. That didn't help your sense of modesty. But you did want to hold onto them. You had just bought them. Comfortable, maximum support without any tightness, with a slight push-up effect. A model from the JOR brand, no longer available for purchase. You have scoured the Web. The ER chief examined your nether regions. The pretty nurse with blond hair was still there. So you tried to put a brave face on.

"We have to see if a projectile has remained in your stomach," the doctor announced.

He turned you over and started to palpate around the abdominal and pubic area. Then he suddenly stopped, immediately giving you back all your dignity of a rocker and big, wild man, even dressed only in tattered boxers and boots.

"Too muscular. Get him to the CAT scan!"

As Seen from Outside: VIII

On November 13, I was in Paris, but wasn't.

I had a very important appointment at half past noon. The kind of meeting where you play all your cards, with your guts on the table.

Under the heaters, we ate on the patio.

Two beers. A steak across from me. An omelet in front of me.

As the red juices spread over the too-thin edges of his plate, in the depths of my yolks speckled with unseemly whites, I was on the lookout for clues of a solid "Yes" from my eminent interlocutor.

I could only find herbs punctuating my eggs.

We ordered another beer. I was hoping that that "Yes" would rise up out of the mist.

The man knew he had a hold on me. That he was holding a pivotal chapter of my life hostage in the middle of that froth that I saw was quickly going flat at the bottom of our rounded glasses.

The powerful always leave the table first, so he had to get going, of course, and kept his answer preciously under his turtleneck.

He nevertheless tried to be elegant by making up for my dashed reaction with percentages.

But a positive response withered down by 20 percent is not chivalry. It's torture.

He was the captain of the shining ship. I was the

swab awaiting orders, sitting on a wobbly chair under a circle of sneering gulls.

My eyes looked at my feet, tied down with twenty pounds of hope.

The captain cast my anchor there with a smirk. I saw him get ready to leave, but didn't stay.

I had another appointment with another director. The man I had married and who had divorced me no more than seven months earlier. The last time we had seen each other was at the courthouse. He had straw on his sweater; there were crumbs on mine. The breakup had been just as fast as the union. Fifteen minutes. It was the months before and after that were endless.

Gallons of regret turned into wine. To withstand that postmortem discussion, I had to have a lot to drink. There is always lots of life in death. That's where it begins, and it is only nourished by death. At any rate, in the lives I've led, I've seen my share of deaths. Too many.

I found him handsome. I found him old. I stared at his wrinkles and avoided his eyes. His voice broke through my eardrums because it was too suave. We had just finished off wine jug number one. He wanted to talk to me about her and that hot-air balloon they were making together, but I swatted the conversation away with a wave of my hand.

We had once been like clouds and floated across the sky together. I couldn't, didn't want to, and already knew it all anyway. Her first name, her fine chin, and what she did. I knew that she was the one who had sewn the black shirt, dappled with little brown leaves, that covered his chest.

Luckily, I wasn't in love with him and didn't force myself. That day, I had but one thing to say, but that definitely needed a second jug of wine.

I would have liked him to reassure me. Or at least lie to me.

"Today, you know, about the separation. There's only one thing I miss, that I miss a lot."

"What's that, Eglantine?"

"Our dimension, Clément. The one that opened up all the others for us."

I poured myself another glass, both for the alcohol and as a way to hamper any possible reaction from my former husband with my frail gestures.

"When I think about that, I see an empty chair too, Eglantine."

An empty chair. That changed absolutely nothing, but that changed absolutely everything. So we had another glass.

We didn't have the choice. Our wedding bands were tattoos that we wore every day, and would wear every day until our last. I hate mine as much as I love it. When friends advised laser treatment to make mine go away, I wondered how swapping writing for a scar could make it *all* go away. The math is wrong. It's not subtraction. It's multiplication.

And then there was that ring. That mark around your finger and over time. I think I loved it more than I hated it, first of all because he had the same mark.

Because I found him handsome before finding him old, I had to go. To imitate that strength that others grasp.

I was almost swaying under the weight of the wine, but demanded maximum control from my legs. You must always be at the height of beauty when you see your exes again. Beyond sublime for the ex.

A perfect gait, every hair perfectly in place, and a tantalizingly revealing top so he could slip all the regrets he would never confess to between my breasts.

Given how I couldn't say hello to him, I didn't manage to say goodbye. How can you kiss the cheek of someone whose lips you devoured for so many years? Decked out in Merlot red, I asked Clément, without giving him the benefit of a question, to hold out his arms parallel to the ground. And I leaped into them. *Bam*, I gave him a blushing-bride kiss right on the lips and went my way.

Now I could stagger.

After I'd done everything to beat it back, I felt the alcohol level shoot up all of a sudden once my ex's back was turned. But the alcohol wasn't alone in my bloodstream. It stared the stage with a chemical that had just been administered to me, barely a few weeks back.

Lithium. A poison to do me good, it would seem.

Alcohol and lithium. I didn't really know who I was in the thick of all that, but remembered I was putting up my mother that night. As if my day hadn't already been big enough.

I got to the house about fifteen minutes before her. I needed some extra courage. So rather than serving myself some water, I opened another bottle of wine.

I think that I was soaked in neither the alcohol nor those new invading molecules but in a wash of emotions. My head was heavy, my ideas too. My mother rang the doorbell.

Sweet and blue, we were thirty minutes away from the first rumors of the drama. I had been disconnected all day long and had no idea that Erwan was in the crossfire of this drama.

I poured my mother some lemon juice and hid my red wine in a glass that was deeper blue than hers. Nobody is as wary of alcohol as my mother. Alcohol is the demon.

We talked about those nasty encounters, that important appointment and its waffling captain. I was drinking discreetly but had no room left. From that moment on I don't remember much, but think I went to go throw up.

The telephone rang. I answered without really knowing who I was talking to.

That voice, the voice of my partner, talked about a certain Bataclan (which I only knew by name), Erwan, terror. I didn't understand.

My mother passed me the online news and nervously repeated to me the same things that that voice had whispered in my ear. I didn't understand. I understood the sounds of our language, but only that.

On her face blurred by my lack of understanding, I saw tension, cheeks that puckered, hands that fluttered about, and a furrowed brow. Ever since the *Charlie Hebdo* incident, I had boned up on a thousand and one hours of documentaries on the Islamic State. When I stumbled on the images of the execution of the policeman Ahmed, I fell to the floor. I stayed there on my knees, my head in my hands and my eyes filled with tears, for half an hour.

Calling his executioner "Boss" went deep into my innards. I couldn't breathe anymore.

It wasn't a man who had been murdered. It was all humanity.

"Really? Well, I'll give him a call then!"

"No. They don't need you now! Go to bed, Eglantine. You are out of it!"

"So, I'll send a text message."

"What are you going to write?"

"His name. That's all!"

I still didn't understand. I needed to urgently reconnect with his name. Erwan.

Erwan. That man who was also tattooed in my flesh. The very first.

...

I had decided to etch his name on my skin for his thirty-ninth birthday, but that morning I wasn't expecting him to wake me up to take me with him to a secret spot. During the whole trip, I was thinking that his parents might have offered him a new sports car, and that he needed me to drive it back. That was my only lead. But I knew that Erwan was able to give somebody else a gift for his own birthday. Given becoming the gift.

My appointment on the tattoo couch was at 3 pm. I had to be on time.

Around 1 pm, we were at the cemetery, where my father was buried. Did Erwan want to salute him in particular that day? I didn't think so.

I had trouble finding my father's grave. Erwan didn't.

He kneeled in front of it and asked my father for my hand in marriage.

The dead speak so softly that I had to answer in his stead.

Erwan didn't know it at the time, but two hours afterward I would also give him a piece of my arm.

...

I can't go to sleep without having an alcohol-free warm beverage. Rarely to drink it, but always there to reassure me. That night, I was unable to carry it to my nightstand. I fell onto my bed with it and scathed myself.

"Ow!"

"Well, you see, that's hardly surprising! You can't even stand straight. You can't even see where you're going!"

"Any news?"

"Shut up, Eglantine. Go to sleep!"

I went to sleep. I didn't even know what news I was getting.

Around 6 am, back-masked shrieks made me jump from my sheets still wet with herbal tea, but I still didn't understand. I plugged in my telephone, battery drained by missed calls in the night. My mother was already up. I had no idea what to say to her. I still didn't understand everything but suddenly realized that I had been absent on the exact day when I really needed to be there. My telephone, which I had unknowingly left silent, spat a hundred pings at me.

That's when I understood almost everything.

To imagine such a thing was unimaginable.

I remembered a documentary on lesbian mothers that I caught midway with Erwan. A woman was going to give birth. Her partner at the clinic was being interviewed.

"You're committed to being here despite your deathly fear of blood and hospitals?"

"There are some important appointments in life that, if you miss them, deprive you of a whole experience. Your absence at that exact moment is irreparable. Even if you had always been there before and do everything right now to make up for that unfortunate absence. For that appointment, you weren't there."

A call. It was the hospital in Créteil. Actually, no. It was Erwan.

His voice first caressed me because I recognized it. It was truly his.

A bullet from a Kalashnikov, a shortened concert, blood, bodies, legs, jaws, dozens of eyes open yet dead. He stopped his both rushed and bare-bones description and asked me to call right away his closest friends who had fretted all night long.

What?

What?

WHAT?!

"I didn't have my phone, and your number is the only one I know by heart. So I called you during the night, but you must have been asleep."

Yes, I must have been asleep. Here you have the lone inhabitant of our country who was asleep that night. That was me.

I don't know if my feeling was closer to pure shame or infinite horror. Yes, there you have it. While Erwan was getting himself shot in the midst of guttural shrieks, heaps of bewilderment, floods of iridescent red, and shredded metal guitar strings, I was asleep. Passed out.

Erwan survived ISIS. But how was I going to get over my absence at that exact moment? I don't know.

The alternative would seem to be to concentrate on being alive. Erwan is alive.

The problem with that alternative is that questions mount right behind it.

And what if he had not survived?

And what if he had survived but, I don't know,

paralyzed, even quadriplegic, with the weight of my absence sitting on his lifeless lap?

Confronted with these questions, behind the window, I remain standing and avoid my reflection.

19

WE ARE GOING TO TAKE CARE OF YOU. Everything is under control. As you were waiting for the CAT scan (or was this before being examined?), one or two cops questioned you, adopting touching oratorical precautions.

The surroundings grew hazy, lighter. Movement broke up into flakes. Effects from the drugs or your whole being letting go?

CAT scan. A pampering team. Tears were in some eyes. You would see them ten days later for another ride in the machine, and they would tell how you couldn't stop joking, how you made them all laugh. One injection, many injections. You remember a sharp pain and a sudden loss of sensation in your right leg—a power outage. You don't really know what happened afterward. You think that you went through your first operation. You're not sure. Everything got mixed together. The timeline isn't fixed in your mind. You could check in your medical file, but that would be cheating, right? Yes, an initial intervention to most likely stop the hemorrhaging and assess the damage. "Embolization of the 'artery of shame'"[11] was

---

11 Translator's note: The French term for the internal pudendal artery, which supplies the genitals with oxygenated blood.

written somewhere. You quickly checked the Internet because you needed some answers, and then … a fright.

You let yourself be hauled around. Everyone was so kind. When a stretcher-bearer took you up to the eleventh floor and the intensive care unit, night was nearing its end.

It was a small room, behind the reception desk. There was a young brunette next to your bed. She introduced herself as Delphine. Night-shift nurse. You dozed off. You woke up with wires, catheters, ivs, and tubes all over the place. That disgusted you, frightened you, distressed you. You would have liked to rip everything off as heroes do, get up and get out of there, ready for new adventures. Either you were a real sissy, or we have to rethink the credibility of Hollywood cinema. You hate hospitals. You get queasy when you get your blood pressure or an X-ray taken. You almost pass out from the slightest prick of a needle. A little less than two months after the Bataclan, you went to a dentist. You'd told yourself that given what you had gone through, you didn't fear anything anymore. Barely seated in the chair, you were paralyzed by fright. Impossible to open your mouth. The dentist told you that she had seen cases of this, but the likes of you … She barely managed to finish cleaning your teeth. One image has always haunted your mind. An operation on your tonsils. You were six. A glob of spongy, blood-soaked magma came out of your mouth at the end of pliers held by the doctor. You remember his fury. He balled you out! Your panic almost drove you insane. You haven't been back to the dentist since. You should. We'll see.

On the other side of the partition, a twenty-four-year-old kid had a bullet wound that went from top to bottom. Lungs punctured. Spinal column hit. He could never walk again.

You hate hospitals. You are a wimp. You tried to negotiate your way out of a urinary catheter. Failed attempt. You would quickly learn that nurses always win. And that a hospital doctor or surgeon rarely makes the rounds without the company of four or eight interns. You asked them if you could leave Monday. They all burst out in fits of laughter. You have always been an optimist—you may even have always overestimated yourself.

When you asked questions about your injuries, everybody skirted the subject. Was it because they didn't know or because they wanted to spare you the truth? You couldn't move your right leg. Would you have after-effects? Nobody wanted to venture a guess. Or it was serious, and they didn't think you were in a state to hear the truth? Would I be able to get a hard-on one day? You didn't dare ask, but you knew where you were hit. You couldn't feel much from your butt or your perineum. Or, more worrisomely, from your penis or testicles.

Would I be able to get a hard-on one day? A primal, essential question that had already started to haunt you. And that was just the beginning.

Saturday, November 14, the first visitors: Jeanne, with Bertrand and Charlotte. Those who had spent all night on the watch, looking for news, informing friends and family, without faltering, without fail. The ones who only learned at four o'clock in the morning that you were alive, more than two hours after your message to Poopy (who only got it in the early morning hours), more than four hours after the beginning of the attack. You hadn't thought about calling your own number. You became aware of this idiocy months afterward. Your phone was at Jeanne's place, but *you had not thought about calling yourself*. Extraordinary suffering makes us shrivel up around ourselves. A less admirable explanation would be that your unconscious wanted others to worry about you.

Jeanne and your friends were beautiful. They were heroes. Victims as well. You loved them.

As you had begged over the telephone, Jeanne brought you the manuscript of *Marguerite n'aime pas ses fesses* (Marguerite Doesn't Like Her Butt), your novel set to hit the shelves in four months time. That was your first request when she asked you what you needed. To correct your text. You knew that without that distraction, you would blow a gasket.

They took you down to the OR. You waited in the hallway in front of the swinging doors. You could not move from your bed on wheels. You knew nothing about the scope of the damage in your flesh. You hurt. You were wondering if they had forgotten about you. "We've had some complications," the nurses coming out of the operating room repeated to you at regular intervals. You wondered if they weren't in the middle of repairing your fellows in misfortune. You weren't angry at anybody, just at yourself for having forgotten to bring something to read. There was nothing there. No magazines in the waiting room. It was cold. You hung around for four hours. You only remember the anesthesiologist in the OR. "You are going to go to sleep in …"

After an operation on your digestive tract, you didn't have the right to eat or drink. You asked if that was a joke. No. You managed to get the right to wet your lips and your mouth, then to spit the water out. "Don't swallow anything, okay? I'm trusting you." First of all, you are an army brat. Obedience flows in your veins. And second of all, you were too freaked out to disobey a medical order.

Visitors. Your parents (who had just got back from Vietnam), Delphine, Fred, Guillaume, Philou, Hubert, Manuel, and Emilie. You don't remember who came or in what order anymore, but it was good. Tears upon tears. Smiles. It was so fucking good! Why not do that every day? Why not every moment of our lives? Why do we have to wait for tragedies? For a few years now you have decided to say "I love you" to those you love, to say it when things are good, when things are beautiful, when things are touching. To express your feelings. To try to be kind and well-meaning against the reigning cynicism and your proud, selfish core. That has changed everything. Love all around. Giving it. Receiving it. That has changed everything. Too bad for the cold fish.

As Seen from Outside: IX

That Friday the 13th couldn't have started any better.

With an evening spent with friends, oysters, champagne, and a playful mood in an apartment near the Place de la République.

Everything changed with a call to one of the party-goers to announce an explosion at the Stade de France, the incidents on the café patios, and gunshots said to be fired at the Bataclan.

"Fuck, Fouch[12] is at the Bataclan."

Anxious text messages. No answers.

The unthinkable was occurring.

We didn't know anything. A chaos of news. People running madly in the streets.

"No news of Fouch."

We were stunned, without really realizing what had happened.

We started to down our drinks in one chug. We were together, but everyone was alone, lost, and isolated with his or her representations of horror, imagining the unimaginable, and, as time went on, the number of victims rose. We were drunk. With desperate,

---

12 This absurd and unattractive nickname dates from my college years at Aix-en-Provence. Its origins can be attributed to Jean-Mi, aka John Mou, who, hearing that I was born in Clermont-Ferrand, exclaimed one night, "Oh, so you're a 'Fouchtra' [an interjection from that town's region, Auvergne]!"

raging, powerless, and tormented drunkenness. We were getting blasted. That was all we could do.

Anger mounted. On the way back home, biking down the deserted streets of a battered city, I screamed, "Bunch of cocksuckers!" at the top of my lungs.

I ended up going home. Still with no news from Fouch. It was one in the morning.

Connected to social media. Jeanne had created a Facebook group and informed us that Erwan did not have his cell phone on him. We were still without any news.

I opened a bottle of red wine, and I drank alone.

At three in the morning, still no news.

I fell into a deep, drunken sleep.

I woke up with a jerk at five. Went to check the Facebook group. "Erwan has been wounded. He has taken a bullet. He is at the hospital, but he is alive."

I threw up everything, and then I cried.

A visit to the hospital on Sunday.

For twenty-four hours, a media loop of terrified faces.

But everything remained abstract and unreal, because that surpassed all understanding. We couldn't "think" about what had occurred.

There was one priority. Go see Fouch at the hospital.

He welcomed us, smiling, drugged, and also exalted to be alive, and in one piece.

He had taken a bullet in the ass.

"That makes him twice as much an asshole," Jean-Mi told me over the phone. We broke out into a nervous fit of laughter.

The first thing he told us was that "I'm lucky. The young man next door, 25 years old, has a punctured lung. Spinal cord was hit. He will never walk again."

That was the first concrete moment of realization.

Then he told us about his passage through Hell.

That was exactly what I told myself, "My buddy spent four hours in Hell, and he came back."

Some of his words grab me, paralyze me, terrorize me, chill me.

That was the first story I had heard, well before all the articles and accounts, well before the victims' portraits in *Le Monde*, and it was the only one I will remember.

The whole time he was telling his story, I was looking at his hands.

Erwan was in a hospital smock, with tubes and IVs everywhere, like after an operation.

The only difference was his hands.

There was dry, brown blood on his fingers, encrusted around each fingernail.

Yes, when we get operated on, our hands are clean.

Not here. His hands were dirty with a nightmare, with his blood and that of others, like indelible ink. The stigmata of horror.

At that moment, for me, the attacks of November 13 became real.

I could not turn my eyes away from his hands.

That image was going to haunt me for a long time. It haunts me still.

I told him that he had to write about what had just happened, not necessarily for it to be published, but because it had to get out. To find an escape hatch, to exorcise that noise, that smell, those shouts. To create movement in the tale of those four hours of total silence and stillness, stifling his suffering and playing dead.

Fifteen days ago, we had another party with friends in that apartment at République. We hadn't been back there since. We all had the idea to do so, a collective need to break the spell.

It was once again on a Friday.

This time, the buffet table had been set up in another part of the room, in another direction. Intentionally.

20

D AY 3. Current power rating: Weak. Status: Drugged up. Avatar: Vegetable. You understood that: You were not ready to leave. You understood that: If the bullet had too nastily fractured your hip bone, that would mean forty-five days of total immobilization. You understood that: You were not going to be able to send your employer the rewritten text for Monday. You understood that: You would be on the fringes of the world from now on.

Passive. Assisted.

A drugged-up vegetable.

Day 3. Anchors aweigh to a new world. Your bed set sail. They moved you. They rolled you over. They pushed you through doors, waiting for the elevator. They took you down, through hallways, still more swinging doors. They turned. Farewell 11th-floor ICU. Greetings to the Digestive Surgery Unit of the 4th floor. There was chattering upon your arrival. With one voice more high-pitched than the others. "Hello, I'm Babeth." A nice smile. There was a problem about the room you were going to move into. Was it ready or not? Unclear. You were expected, nonetheless. Babeth pushed you into Room Number 2. It was free. "He'll be happy there. At least he'll be all alone."

You didn't realize right away the gift Babeth had given you by not respecting the room planning. The vast majority of patients were in double rooms, with all the problems that come with the fellowship of the catheter. You didn't realize it right away, because the lighting was pallid, the walls stark white. The night lurked behind glum windows with their piss-colored drizzle. Because this room change confirmed that you were not going to leave the Henri-Mondor Hospital anytime soon. You still couldn't get it up. At any rate, a tube was sticking out of your dick, its end attached to a plastic sack. So, all the better you couldn't.

Anchors aweigh to a new, morbid world. Sad decor. Cold. An unfathomable loneliness blindsided you that night, torpedoed you with a dark melancholy.

So, there you were, captain of a motionless, 30-inch-wide vessel, with its reclining function, modular sidebars, and an IV pole on the left. You could not leave the ship. The sea was swarming with sharks. You had to stay flat on your back. There was a dismal sea of time to cross. At least you didn't have a tube in your nose anymore. They called it a "respiratory assist device." There were the needles, however, and the constant pain, however, that broke up your sleep at irregular yet tight intervals. No way to turn over to your left; no way to move your left arm too much at the risk of ripping out the tubes. You slept in time slots of two hours maximum.

And then there was *Marguerite* … Like a lighthouse of misfortune. And that red pen that strikes out, strikes out, strikes out, and rewrites in the calm of the night.

It had barely been fifteen days since your editor and you met to talk about the publication of your novel. He had liked the text. You had liked the man. He kindly offered to push back the publication date, set for April 14, 2016. "Your decision is mine," he had written to you a few days after your hospitalization. Charge ahead, guy! Charge! You only had *Marguerite* ... to forget your ransacked flesh, a possible future without erections, the needles, the pills, the bandages, the various sacks to which you were linked. We had to charge ahead. If not, your vessel would sink, and the sharks of neurasthenia would rip your mournful soul to shreds. Write, to make out safe harbor from the crow's nest. And read. Everything that was given to you. Everything that anyone would bring. Reading and writing. The two poles of your existence. You could live alone. You would even prefer it. But not without books. Not without literature. Not without a pen.

Our historian has identified certain high points of this start of the journey.

The first slice of crispbread. Crispbread is delicious. You had forgotten its taste. Highly underestimated, crispbread is. All because of Swedish rusks? So, those Vikings weren't happy enough killing off our furniture craftsmen and strangling our thriller writers to death? Those barbarians had to reduce our crispbread industry[13]

---

13 While there were more than three hundred crispbread makers in France in the 1970s, there were only six left in 2017, according to Wikipedia.

to crumbs too? We, the French, call them *biscotte*, from the Italian *biscotto*, "twice cooked." The medieval Latin *biscottum* appears as of 1218 in Modena, according to the *Dictionnaire historique de la langue française*. After four days without swallowing a thing, not even water, seized with gratitude, you relish the best *biscotte* of your entire life. A return to the wheat fields of your childhood, where you would gleefully pick a head of wheat and munch on the husked grain. A return to breakfast tables where the challenge consisted in buttering the crispbread without breaking it. Some hold that one must always place one on top of another. However, the sole result of that doubtful strategy is a doubling of the risk of breakage.

The removal of the urinary catheter. Which should have been a moment of liberation, to put some wind in your sails even if there was no land on the horizon. You dreaded it, of course. (You preferred just forgetting that it was even there.) "Don't worry. It's virtually painless," the nurse said with a smile. Everybody on that hospital floor heard you scream. You even wondered if that didn't hurt more than the bullet.

The reconnection to your messages. An outpouring of love, friendship, and thoughtfulness. Support. Encouragement. Concern. Curiosity. It was sometimes unhealthy: mobs of new virtual friends were lining up at the door in hopes of an appreciative click. You didn't want any television or newspapers on board your raft, to be spared the media gales that you suspected were battering dry land. Nevertheless, ill winds know how to blow through the slightest crack and hit your starboard side by surprise. An abundance of messages from journalists—the international media, acquaintances of acquaintances, and friends of virtual friends. "So-and-so gave me your contact info." Those little rascals who managed to find you. Even friends from real life. With the arrival of a scoop, breaking news, and an exclusive eyewitness report, mouths were watering everywhere, and you had to bail out your ship.

No TV. No newspapers. At the hospital, you were cut off from all news other than your own. Dosages, diagnostics, needles, an x-ray at 2 pm. A stretcher-bearer would come to get you.

It was easy to imagine. The big headlines, with the shocking photos of blood-soaked survivors, faces twisted with pain and fear. Stuffed with news up to your eyeballs. Horror. Carnage. Massacre. War.

It was easy to imagine. The television channels' special reporters, serious, stodgy, repeating in a loop the numbers of victims, wounded, shooters. Stalking them down as if you were right there. Barbarians at our gates.

It was easy to imagine. Microphones stuck into the noses of family members, neighbors, survivors. Shocked, shaking, moved. It was terrible, horrible, unthinkable, unimaginable, awful. What kind of a world are we living in? Some proffer in hushed voice that they had it coming.

It was easy to imagine. The solemn, noble expressions, stiff and ponderous. With some, traces of sadness; others, traces of anger. From our privileged few in the world of politics: "Strike hard against those who came into our land to slash the throats of our sons and daughters!" Sentences that were soaked in blood, just as your face had been for three hours.

Facebook Status—11/16/2015, 9:36 pm

Apologies to those freaked by my (obligatory) silence Friday night. Thanks for the messages of support. Love in motion is beautiful.

I have done nothing heroic or extraordinary.

On the other hand, I swear to you that that young fireman who kept telling me to hold on while, freezing, I swooned in the cold, he's a hero. At the hospital, with that well-meaning efficiency, the smiling interns, the rushing nurses, the joker anesthetist, the physician's assistant who pampered me, the instructive chief of service. All heroes.

On board, the daily routine of slogging on set in. Nurses made the rounds. Day and night shifts. The etched-in-stone times to eat (with increasingly hearty meals). Ears pricked for sounds in the hallway (carts being moved, voices, microwaves running). Steps, soon a visit, soon human presence, to be able to talk, be comforted, solaced. All were saints. Those who took care of you. You loved them, and you told them so. You loved them. Those who chattered and the grouchy ones. Those who hurt you when they gave you a shot and those who were half-naked under their green smocks. Those who were remote and those who joked. Although you'd been cut off for a few days, you even love those who smell of old smoke, like Abdel, who was nervous and uncomfortable the first days. Did he think you were putting everybody in the same boat?

We need more caregivers, need to pay them more, and focus on their professional well-being. Tax speculation. Cap high salaries. Deal with it, let's all just fucking deal with it. But don't let universal health care fail.

Christophe was a good six feet tall and weighed two hundred pounds. He let you hold onto his arm (which was the size of what was left of your thigh), and let you bite him when his partner took your blood twice daily. When you couldn't bite, you'd sing out loud, or break out in a slew of made-up swear words in an invented tongue between Italian and German. Or pretend you had become brave and could *pas de problème* stand the sight of those blue veins in the crux of your elbows.

Charming young women washed your wounds in the furrow between your buttocks. They emptied and rinsed your pee bottles full of urine. (You would learn, while typing these lines, that the precise term, which no one used in the hospital, was "urinal.") No more embarrassment. No more shame. You were constantly naked under your smock. At any rate, your penis and testicles were dead. You couldn't get it up any more. You tried not to think about it.

Myriam, Maïlis, Anne-Sophie, Habib, Bertrand, Isabelle, Brigitte, Jérôme, Delphine, Micheline, Christophe,

Abdel, Laurence, Sophie, Noémia, Carine, Whitney, Gilles, Babeth, Laurine, Cynthia, Magalie, Marie, Sophie, Karine, Salma, Sylvie, Johann, Hélène, Valérie, Francesco, and Geneviève. What do they take back home with them after a day next to the ill, invalids, ivs, catheters, the doddering cancer victims condemned to die, the paralyzed, the hacking coughs, the migraines, the pneumonia victims, those with ulcers? Did you think they would just take off their smocks and work shoes and all the day's squalor would stay in the locker? They reassured, smiled, comforted, listened. They got insulted by some patients, and others took them for servants and rang for them to come running. Still others had it in for them because the caregivers were in good health, whereas they were so unwell. There were not enough of them. Sometimes there were not enough sheets to change the beds or enough smocks for the patients. They never let you sense their exhaustion or frustration. They were humanity taking care of its own. In bed, you got worked up thinking about the world that wants to privatize them, make them profitable, make them players in the economy of commodification. Is it that complicated to understand that we need them more than we need communications consultants, advertisers, or financial traders? They respond by talking about the massive health care debt. That we need to compare what is comparable. Take a cold look at reality. That welfare kills, and that it is wrong to live beyond your means. And that it's time to take your shot.

Breaking news!

Taking the bull by both horns, holding onto anything he could get his hands on (that is to say, his IV pole), and casting away the urinal, Erwan has peed all by himself.

The toilets are, of course, but four yards from his bed.

Doctors, interns, and surgeons came to see you once a day. They were without fail in a group. The faces changed from one visit to another. You didn't understand who was who, or who did what. They would fan themselves out at the foot of the bed, ask two or three questions, barely listen to your answers, often nod their heads, rarely make eye contact, confabulate, and make their decisions. An x-ray tomorrow, an electromyography (EMG) as soon as possible, a change of diet, and dosages. Then they would leave almost as if you didn't exist, as if you were only a file. Distance. Avoidance.

The EMG, constantly pushed back, would be your Holy Grail for many days, even if you hadn't really grasped what it was about. Only that that exam would show why your fucking right foot didn't want to move anymore. Where were those vile prickly sensations coming from? Had the bullet hit the sciatic nerve? Or was it a crushed popliteal nerve caused by the person on the floor who was holding onto your legs? You shouldn't have been so impatient. You would find yourself studded with electrodes that shot electricity into your leg. The worst half-hour of your time there. A small insight into what electroshock torture must be like. Six months after your release, a follow-up EMG was planned, to see how your nerves had recuperated. The specialist denied you distractions (music or reading). And then got worked up because of your uncontrollable state of sheer panic. Your tears—out of anger and shame at not being able to control your Super Wuss reactions—turned him against you for good. He threw in the towel. Your recovery would be measured by hunches and not by ohms and amperes.

Facebook Status—11/20/2015, 9:39 pm

The surgeon who repaired me is called Francesco. He's a real bigshot, it seems. The whole staff love him. He's Italian, from Naples, smiling and laughing with a sparkle in his eye.

Tonight, our subject quickly changed from feces to football when he saw the soccer magazine brought by my pal Hubert on the nightstand. We compared the new post-Benitez Napoli team to Rudi's Roma players. We brought up Higuaín's moves, players only focused on scoring, Pogba, Verratti. We also, of course, talked about Pirlo.

"We should watch a match together this weekend," I told him.

He laughed.

"I'll make you pasta," he answered. "That's my specialty. I really master making pasta. Maybe more than surgery!"

Francesco didn't tell you any more about your theoretical recovery than the other specialists. But at least, unlike his hurried peers, he was completely present when he was in your room. He demanded that you inform him of the smallest details about the state of your bowel movements. And of when you would first pass gas. The fart would be your unit of measurement of your recovery. Great …

…

You're blocked here. Pen hovering over the notebook. Shit!

…

You were incensed at not being able to call up sensations and details at will. Everything was growing dim. Because you had become an other. Something other than the "I" who had lived through the events. You were no longer the Captain Courageous at one with his bed on wheels. Only flashes remained, which would not have their place in a "work of literature," right? Instants.

Like …

… the desire to sometimes call the nurse in the middle of the night (holding yourself back to not bother her).

… the inflatable ring designed to ease your pain when you sat on your bed that exploded under your ass one morning. With a leap, the nurse almost gouged your eye out with the needle. That would have been the best!

… the moral suffering caused by your damaged senses— swollen, puffy flesh larded down with shredded nerves weren't sending the right news to your brain anymore.

… the first time out of bed, in a wheelchair, to go take a shower, accompanied by Cynthia. You were singing down the hallways as she pushed you along. Then she washed you seated in your wheelchair, working around the ivs. What bliss it was to have hot water flow over your withered body, and through your hair for the first time in four days! Being washed brought you to tears. "We did it, Cynthia. We did it," you couldn't stop repeating to her. "Thank you." One wins the battles one can.

Friends regular bring fresh supplies of optimism, energy, and bravery with their smiles and attention. Jeanne as well, first and foremost. Despite her own traumas, and after having tirelessly coordinated those long hours during which nobody knew if you were alive or dead, she took care of management and logistics, of your car that had stayed parked in front of the Châtellerault train station, of the health care refunds, of the paperwork. Because even if you were immobile and out of the flow of time, the race sailing on off your shores had not stopped. It even seemed more stressful and exhausting than ever. A lot of your visitors seemed more touched and damaged, more traumatized than you were. Sometimes, you were the one who comforted them.

There were those who came right away, crumbling under fatigue and anxiety. Those who came from far away. Those who just dropped by, or happened to be passing through. Those who apologized for coming empty-handed, even though their hearts were overflowing. Those who knew about your little weaknesses—soft caramels and frangipane. Those who brought you books. Those who gave you sweets. Guillaume showed up with a towel, liquid soap, and slippers for your first post-apocalyptic steps. Emma came with a huge stuffed bear, that you would make your confidant and comforter. Myriam sent you a care package. Such a lovely thought! They would come for a few minutes or two hours. Many would gather around the bed, and acquaintances were made. You had unexpected visits, those acquaintances who had been out of contact for a long or short time, but all distraught. An aperitif had even been organized with the old buddies from those days in Aix, with dried sausage, rillettes, pâté, cheese and red wine from Provence. But nobody had remembered the corkscrew. Bill fruitlessly scoured hallways and all the floors to find one. We ended up pushing the corks down the bottleneck. We had the caregivers' permission. They had never seen such a well-looked-after patient. "Your room is full of joy. That's a welcome change. It does us good." Yes, friendship does a body good, and when a stunning blonde nurse sauntered into your kingdom one afternoon offering "A massage?", you knew (you hoped) that Guillaume wouldn't be (too) unhappy with you when you answered, undercutting that fine image of a generous and kindhearted man you like to give, "With pleasure, Ma'am. My friend was just going."

There were almost too many visits some days. You got tired easily. You tried to get the message across without hurting feelings. You sometimes politely sent them away when hints failed. For which of your loved ones would you have gone as far as Créteil? You skirted that question. You were blown away by the generosity of your parents and friends. You would like to share it, loan some to certain rooms, to those stooped, wizened shapes in their beds, to those looks already elsewhere, to those mute, nerve-damaged spirits that collapsed in slobbers or wails in front of a television they didn't even see anymore. Bodies don't get repaired without love. You have to give them a reason to fight. You blessed your jovial nature, that has helped you not weather but accept trials *lightly*. There is a term for this in Occitan: *lou ravi*.

If you have the friends and loved ones you deserve, you are without doubt a better person than you thought.

> **Facebook Status—11/19/2015, 8:30 pm**
> I am learning to become a biped again. It's hard.
> That said, I hope that I am not going to have to learn to become human again.

As Seen from Outside: X

My dear friend,

They are saying, rumors are going around, that you have been wounded. I believe nothing of it, want to believe nothing of it. And yet, now that all of this has become known to me, I must tell you of a dream I had about you that worried me greatly. Are you ready?

Here is the dream:

Voices spoke to me in my sleep. They led me to believe all those horrible things that concerned you. Held in the castle, I only had news of you once the anguish and the night had subsided. Neither expectation, nor hope, nor bruise came to me. Unlike the others, I had averted that first circle of trials, and because of this, my body bore no trace of your martyrdom. I had gone to see you at noon with that friend so dear to us both, in that place where you remained henceforth. A foolish reflex made me buy a Japanese book that you had wanted to photograph, leading me to believe that it would please you.

My manner of lying to you, of pretending that I found myself in the same place as you, and that I was suffering with you, did not seem to affront you. I was relieved to see you in such a state. You seemed brand new.

In my dream, we talked for a long time, recalling a certain place, I think. A place devoid of any link to what had become, for us, the root of a hope and the shape of a faded tie. Many other strange elements enhanced this vision. Your body. Our circle of friends, with that odd idea that we needed to break a curse. Your broken body, made of a mix of fresh and dried blood. I was most likely frightened by this vision. After which you told me you particularly liked my redone face even if, I think, you were talking about someone other than myself, but I could no longer hear you. My inability to read your lips was in no way rewarded, but for that pebble that you described to me, and that had saved your life, which you revealed to me. From that moment on, I felt once more the tale, and your body seemed to me like a stone cross on a wayside. And then that question you posed, "Is your mouth one that would hoard the smile of another?" It was at that moment that I awoke, most likely in a shroud, in the midst of the night.

My dear friend, it may occur that, one day, people would pretend that I be nothing to the other, and that he be nothing for me. It may happen that evil people say you are nothing to me. Believe nothing of that, I beg of you. Are we not tied together by this long friendship, and also by our circle of friends? What would we be in the opposite case, if not the blind sum of our encounters, and the fleeting shape of our comings and goings that, before the murders, we called existence?

It happened that we both thought that we would grow from this. For you, yes. There is no doubt in seeing it thusly. I, for my part, remain the poor sinner you know.

Concerning the murders, I have no idea how to talk about them. You are not ignorant of the fact that among my other infirmities is my lack of opinion about anything. We sometimes discussed the meaning we could give to the world, but you, wiser and more committed, always cut to the quick of the matter. (Like that time, you remember, when, drunkenly leaving the Globo, stumbling through the waning haze of the Châteauroux night, my voice became much too loud.)

And if we must characterize all of this as flaws in my character, as goes your own, I implore you to please forgive me. If you, through the infinite goodwill that I know in you, still wish to keep our friendship, I would hope that you would grant me one final request: to seek out our companions' forgiveness of me, and most importantly, the highly precious forgiveness of our friend who survived the cannon's blow.

You know more than anyone else that if I sometimes cry too readily, I rarely do so when the storm is blowing at our doorstep. Until now, you have never held this against me, preferring to hold back my booming laughter. I am always outside, on the lookout for you and enjoying your faraway delight. What I see is that you, and our friend as well, have done more than survive it all.

There you have, my very dear friend, the oddities that wandered through my night, and the parade of maudlin thoughts that went with them. I do hope that you have not suffered so from their meeting, which I have very lightly romanticized to give them a consistency that my memory could not offer.

I wish you all the best and can barely contain my impatience to hold you soon in my arms and giggle with you about this whimsy, seated around one of those fat, roasted fowl whose tender flesh we both hold so dear.

I hope to see you soon, my very dear friend, and fare thee well, relieved that all has truly been for the best.

Your very devoted,
Anc Le Damneur

21

YOU MADE ACQUAINTANCE WITH YOUR DEATH, lying on the floor of the Bataclan. Now you were meeting your upcoming old age, lying crippled on your hospital bed. The face-to-face meeting with your finitude was just as powerful as the one with your final act. Progress was made. Victories invisible to the outer eye. With your will always on the alert.

Your personal trainer, Geneviève, and her assistant Johann took charge of the battle against your horizontal position. One morning, they dressed you in socks, high-top tennis shoes, and a foot brace, helped you up, and then waddled you down the hallway, half held up by crutches. You felt heroic. You were singing and joking with those you passed, with a smile. You cried over this tiny step forward. Then you almost fainted. We can't imagine everything that staying upright demands. You went through hell because of the bruises and the flagging flesh and tendons caused by your immobility. You had to give in after two or three minutes the first few times.

The day hustled and bustled, shimmied and shook from the moment the sun rose, promising interactions and surprises. But right after the last rounds of the day shift, silence fell. At night there would be one, maybe two check-ins. Efficient. The nurses were responsible for many rooms. Sometimes you wanted to hold them up to chat. Their attitude did not allow for that. You didn't want to risk being snubbed. You knew that for them you were just "2." There was one really pretty nurse with walnut-colored skin. As a basic male, you ogled her breasts, her butt, her panties when you could. Out of reflex. But that had no effect on you. The absence of mental stimulation panicked you almost as much as your inert genitalia. Which had an explanation. And what if you would never want to lose yourself between the thighs of a woman again? And what if you would never react again to a round backside? Wait! Just a minute! Let me take a gander at your ... But she had already left.

"Have you done 4?", her colleague asked her in the hallway.

"No, 4 is a pain."

Rather than diving into grammatical absurdities, you grabbed your red pen and worked out your frustration on *Marguerite* ...

The day bustled. The night, that scurvy silence, would buckle down to drain all remission. The consciousness of yourself would spread out and multiply. Pain would settle in, freed of that pride that would make you grit your teeth in the light of day and strut your stalwart stuff. What good is it to keep a stiff upper lip when there's no one around to see it? The darkness had nothing to do with it. It was solitude that frittered you away, that made you slip away and come uncorked, mixed up in the tubes and the sheets and the blankets. It sharpened the discomfort of that narrow little bed where sleep did not feel welcome.

Your backside had the entry and exit wounds from the bullet, plus the scars from the operation conducted by Francesco. It stung. It itched. It burned. It bothered you. You had diapers, compresses, and bandages to change, because the lesions would ooze. Stuff would seep out. That was only natural, because fluids were draining out. Scarring is an organic process. You hurt. Your stomach was hard and swollen. Your body would send jumbled and contradictory signals to your brain. At night, what else was there to listen to in your isolation but those little rodents?

It was an entire expedition to traverse those three yards to the toilet seat, with the iv mast and tubes (you had move everything from the other side of the bed). With your sluggish leg, you had to hop there (once, you slipped and miraculously caught yourself against the wall). It was grueling. Grueling to get seated, grueling to stay seated, grueling to get back to the bed. So every time you would stay a long time on the toilet, awaiting liberation. You couldn't feel your balls anymore. Your perineum looked like a cauliflower. Pins and needles and electrical prickling in your nerves. Your muscles either didn't obey or obeyed badly. You got furious. You cried. You railed. And nothing would come. You were scared to go too far and burst open your brand-new scars. Your intestines, traumatized and crumpled up, were not responding to your calls.

At night, you would talk to yourself. You would encourage yourself. You would motivate yourself. You would rant at yourself. You gave yourself permission to be proud of yourself, and to cry to irrigate your courage. Nobody knows anything about those monologues that weave us together. Over fifteen days of hospitalization, you would see fifteen sunrises. Each time with the same gratefulness. Then the day would begin to shimmy and shake, and the devotion, attention, and care of the whole staff would come pouring down upon you. Those people without golden parachutes, without vacation homes, without stock options. Who take public transport, grumble through the traffic jams as they head off on vacation and groan through the jams coming back at the wheel of their car bought on the installment plan. Those people who won't have a Rolex at fifty, and will work until they are seventy. Somebody has to pay for those golden parachutes, those dividends, and those stock options.

By now you were determined to take a shower every day, all by yourself. By leaning on a crutch and against the walls. While dragging your little, hanging, plastic bags behind you. Francesco examined you frequently. He was amazed by the scarring and general progress of your wound. He asked you if you had passed gas (*Si? Bene, bene!*). You still couldn't get a hard-on. You got worried for the thousandth time about how many days a biped can last without going to the toilet. (For you, normally, it was zero. You had always had easy bowel movements.

Might as well say that the record you were then setting was not going to get broken any time soon.)

"Mr. Larher," Francesco said, raising a finger, falsely pedantic, with his ever so-strong Italian accent, "Be sure of one thing: Poop always wins in the end."

Conversation with many, Facebook—11/21/2015, 10:42 pm
He saw that Erwan had been patient.

He saw that Erwan had been respectful of his bowel movements.

He saw that Erwan had farted at a good and pleasing rhythm.

And thus, on the Eighth Day, He opened the Holy Sphincters.

And how are things in your head?"

"My head? I got shot in the ass."

(Upraised eyes.)

"Yes, I know. But … do you think about it? Do you have nightmares? Do you have panic attacks?"

No. No, nothing like all that. No night sweats either. You were at the wrong place at the wrong time. You are a miracle, not a victim. Iblis, Efrit, and Saala had nothing against you personally. Nothing to make you hide away in fear. Poppy has multiple sclerosis. You can't cure that. You never forgot that.

"You are rationalizing."

Well, of course. You kept hearing that you were a monster for not waking up screaming every night. You felt normal, but you looked for explanations, because it would seem that you were not so normal. (*Lou ravi?*)

"What you lived through is not normal."

"I didn't see anything. Only heard. As much as a pebble could hear, that is."

"But it's still traumatizing, right?"

What traumatized you was that you didn't know if you would one day have a hard-on. Decency and pride still keep you from speaking of it to anyone who had not taken the Hippocratic oath. But that fear was taking up all the room and squashing down the others. As for your leg, skilled experts seemed to diagnose no after-effects because the bullet had not touched the sciatic nerve. As for your digestive system's evacuative function, Francesco deduced that we were on track to be cured. The subject that nobody broached was your future erectile function. If you had to have nightmares, they would have focused on your undone manhood. At any rate, you have to sleep to have a nightmare.

When you thought about your so-called monstrosity, you suspected that your brain had turned on a self-protection mechanism. It had gone into safe mode. With an automatic switch to defend itself from the unthinkable. So why try to drill into these hidden apparatuses when no symptoms were rising to the surface? Under the pretext that you *should* be suffering? That having lived through "that" would *necessarily* leave marks and come back again one day? Maybe "that" will never come back. Maybe the brain is so subtly constructed that it had already done its job. Assimilate. Digest. Switch turned on again. Life goes on.

There was another survivor of the massacre two doors down from you, a little worse off than you were, but nothing irreparable. Guillaume was at the concert with his wife, also wounded, but nothing too serious either. They had children. For him, the event marked a turning point. As soon as he got out, he explained to you enthusiastically, ecstatically, he was going to change his life. Dump his job, which was not fulfilling him. He felt exploited. Dump Paris and start all over again. Build another existence using happiness as the mortar.

"You too?" he asked while lunching in your room.

No. You were happy in your custom-fitted, well-adjusted life, even if you sometimes had to tighten your belt toward the end of the month. You had made the choice to flip everything around fifteen years earlier. To leave behind the music industry with its symbolic, social, and financial bonuses to put writing at the center of your daily schedule. To leave that self-centered slacker personality behind and try to be more attentive to others and to the world (never back down from these efforts). To leave Paris behind. The path had sometimes been steep but always rewarding, interspersed with amazing encounters and rich experiences. You were not going to try to "get the most out of life" any more than before, because you couldn't see how that would be possible, you explained to Guillaume. You did not add that, on the other hand, you could see very well how you could get less out of life if your soldier could no longer stand at attention in front of Venus. Guillaume needed to talk about November 13 and its consequences. Not you. But you didn't have the heart to deny him your presence, so you listened to him talk. You didn't feel the need to exchange stories with other survivors, to share your feelings in group meetings, associations, "just between us" encounters. When the French government invited you to an homage to the victims, you didn't even answer, because the idea seemed so odd.

"And do you never ask yourself why?" Mme. B asked. "No."

Facebook Status—11/24/2015

Madame B. has a haircut the likes of which I have not seen for a long time. A little bit like the Ken doll, but the feminine version. Where not one hair sticks out, with enough hairspray to pierce another hole in the ozone layer, and of an orangish-brown-stain color. Madame B. has the strict look of a mother superior and a stare, certainly worked out over many years, made odd by the blur between pupil and iris.

During her two first visits, Madame B. (always accompanied by one or two colleagues who simply nod their heads or smile) was clearly disappointed that I had no nightmares or night terrors.

During her third visit, I was doubled over in fits of laughter on my bed, because I'd just shared some stupid jokes with Christophe, one of my nursing assistants, built like a brick shithouse and always smiling, with magical fingers and a great sense of banter. I stayed in the same humor during my appointment with Madame B.

The next morning, she pushed the door to my chamber open again and came in with her two flunkies.

"Can we speak, Mr. Larher?"

"Um ... Sure, but you're not going to come every day, are you?"

A moment of silence.

Madame B. shot her look at me, which made you want to ask pardon for breathing. She sighed and pursed her lips, then shook her head from right to left (her hairdo did not move; that was impressive).

"I am sorry, Mr. Larher. (Yeah, right.) But I think that you are truly too joyful."

You weren't joyful anymore when you thought about your cowboy boots. Without even mentioning how the ruins of your favorite boxer trunks and jeans most likely ended up being thrown away in the ER in the confusion of the evening of the 13th. But your boots!

You had adopted cowboy boots at the Institute for Political Science at Aix-en-Provence, under the influence of the first of your classmates to become a friend, Jean-Mi. He also helped you discover the Velvet Underground and Sonic Youth. All praise to him! He wore them in both summer and winter with a cool attitude that impressed you. At the time, you were getting out of your gothic period and were looking for your next look. Cowboy boots did just the trick during that period of indecision.

You opted for the low-cut model, stopping just above the ankle (unlike Jean-Mi, the ayatollah of the calf-high version). Cowboy boots must have a beveled heel, short enough to make the toe stick up. (You had one or two layers of leather removed from the heel by a cobbler.) They had never left your shoe reserve. You told people that the pair that had disappeared in the maze of Henri-Mondor hospital were twenty-five years old. That was an exaggeration. More like around fifteen years. You got joshed for it sometimes. ("Cowboy boots? Way too tacky!") You were able to give yourself a pat on the back as a trend stockpiler, before they went out of style two years later. Oh, the inconvenience of being faithful.

The model you wore to the Bataclan were rather hard to find. Outside of the particularity of their heels, those boots were pointed (we sometimes talk about a "snip" point) and basic black, with no frills. (Mexicans, those kings of the cowboy boot, have an amazing inclination to over-decorate their boots, sometimes to the point of kitsch.) You had just had them repaired because the original leather sole had split along the ball of the foot, right where they would curve when you walked. The operation had been complicated, and expensive. You were tempted to talk to your insurance agent about it.

A member of the hospital team took off your boots a little after you arrived at Henri-Mondor and put them at the foot of your rolling stretcher. They were still there when you were moved to the 11th floor, to the ICU. You were woozy, half passed-out. They had probably already shot you up with drugs, but you were sure the boots were still there. Was it then, during your transfer to the digestive surgery ward that Tuesday, that they disappeared? Or just before? Your most probable theory, at least the one that gratified your ego the most, was that a fetishist and/or enamored nurse nicked them behind your back. You couldn't believe that it could have been one of your visitors. Among the first, there was Philou, who must be size 13 and only collects horse-related things; Hubert, who only wears Doc Martens: your old pals Fred and Guillaume, who respected the boots too much to commit such larceny—even if they've gone bourgeois and only wear Italian shoes. No, the more you thought about it, the more you suspected an overwhelmed admirer. Which only barely soothed your chagrin.

You set the whole hospital service on the hunt, even the social welfare assistant. All in vain. "You know, there are, alas, a lot of thefts in hospitals," she told you. When people ask you if you have any after-effects from the Bataclan, the impotency comes up first. Then, well before your paranoia, even before the shot-to-hell skinny jeans and boxers (whose tatters, with their potential value as relics, you wouldn't recuperate either), comes your burgled cowboy boots. The worst thing about it is that everybody thinks you are joking.

As Seen from Outside: XI

I was not in Paris the night of November 13–14, 2015.
I was at my parents', in my childhood bedroom. There
were parrots on the wainscoting, on the curtains,
on the drapes. The coat hangers are shaped like
cockatoos. I don't remember why I loved parrots so
much at a moment in my childhood. What I have
known for a long time, on the other hand, is that
during nights of anxiety, those parrots—with their
heads tilted to one side like zombies in a Romero
movie—can become terrifying.

But November 13 started like a fun evening—that
seems like a clumsy memory today. I had just received
a literary award, and I was having a fine glass of wine
with my parents in front of the fireplace. And here's
the funny part, we were talking about Erwan. I didn't
know why my parents were interested in him. They
had only run into him once, at a book fair in Le Mans.
I think they liked his magic tricks, and then the book
about the male personality today left them confused,
yet appreciative. I often giggle inside when I think
that if they had known we had slept together, they
wouldn't have understood his short stories in the
same friendly way.

My telephone was ringing off the hook. Text
and Facebook messages full of congratulations. I
remember saying to my parents, without knowing

what had got hold of me, "Life is great." My parents, who had seen me collapsed in front of them whimpering, "I'll never make it," smiled tenderly with that look of mind-readers that I had always envied them. And then the fine wine and the fire knocked me out. I went up to bed, even if it was very early, something I allowed myself because that parrot room often saw me go to bed at an early hour, something hard to admit afterward if someone were to ask me what I was doing that night of the 13th, because having gone to bed at 9 pm makes me feel like an idiot. Before dozing off, I connected one last time to Facebook and posted "Thanks" right and left. I think I saw something drift by about gunfire at the Stade de France, but that didn't shock me. Or I was too sleepy to click on the link, I don't know. I also noticed that Erwan was heading off to the Bataclan in his cowboy boots. I smiled, dreaming of his rocker array. I thought once again about what he once told me under the Bougival sun when last night's smokes had sapped my strength and I was giving him a hard time because he was off to play squash. I don't remember his words exactly, but they were something like, "Sweetie, at my age, you can't be a rocker and not do some sports. If I get fat, I'd look like stupid fucker, or a pig in three-quarters of my wardrobe." That made me laugh. Even if I most likely thought with a certain anguish that he was much skinnier than I was, and that my twenty-seven years didn't help out matters at all.

Second odd thing. Why does everything become a weird coincidence after the fact? Why is there always something that makes us think about a presentiment? That night, I didn't switch off my cell phone before going to sleep. Which is what I normally do, out of the fear that the EM waves would alter the quality of my sleep, or because I was too often woken up by drunk buddies demanding I meet them *right now* at the other end of Paris. (Something I could understand once I added the consonants they couldn't manage to push through their lips.) The buzzer woke me just as I had dozed off. I noticed while picking up that I had had the time to receive a dozen messages. On the other end of the line Corentin, a long-time friend working in Dubai, was worried—Where was I? How was I? He spoke very quickly, and I answered slowly, whispering. Between the haze of sleep and the parrots staring at me, my brain had trouble getting what Corentin was explaining. Shots fired at the Stade de France, and at the Bataclan, maybe elsewhere. He was notably trying to reach a common friend who was living in the 10th arrondissement and not answering her phone. I reassured him.

"Well, that must be a story of settling scores, right? I can't see why Claire would be mixed up with that business. And the Bataclan is far from her place, and ..."

Erwan's cowboy boots burst into my thoughts. That could have been a shot from an old western, before the camera pans to Clint Eastwood's face. And I froze.

I can't find the first text message I had sent him. What I remembered was that I wrote it before going online, and that it was a rather calm, almost casual message. Something like, "Hope everything's fine. Get back to me? Love."

I imagine that every Parisian recognizes what I received in the meantime. A succession of "Are you okay?" and "Where are you?"

I became aware of the scope of the attacks while cursing the signal that, wouldn't you know it, couldn't completely make it to the parrot room, land of childhood protected from the Internet, only furnishing me information drop by drop. I tried to go to sleep, couldn't manage to, wrote to Erwan again. This time, I was clearly distressed: "Fuck, tell me you're okay."

The night dragged on, both short and slow, punctuated with "Are you okay?"/"Where are you?" And for every friend who reassured me, the names and faces of two or three others welled up, in that abnormally quiet room. So once more, I would write "Are you okay?" in the dark, and wait.

Sometimes, between two messages, I would go to sleep. And in my sleep, I heard my phone chime. The noise would enter into my dream, and my dream would assimilate it, digest it. I dreamed I was alerted by text message that all Paris was safe and sound. Many times, while waking up, I would put my hand on my telephone, persuaded that Erwan had answered.

But there was nothing.

I read on Facebook that he had forgotten his phone at his girlfriend's place, and I told myself to no longer write messages as if I were grasping for somebody's hand in the dark.

That was the first time I had experienced such a situation: where I knew nothing. I had experienced— rarely, admittedly—losing people close to me, but I had always learned of their deaths as a clear fact. No one had ever said to me, "It might be that so-and-so has passed away. Or maybe not. Nobody knows." It was a little bit like the experiment with Schrödinger's cat. For several hours, Erwan was both alive and dead. It was crazy the number of thoughts that cropped up over that time.

The night of November 13 marked a year and a half since the last time I had seen Erwan. We had run into each other at Le Mans, as usual, but that year he did a split-second return trip because the bookstores had forgotten to order his books. So that didn't count. The last time that I had really spent time with him, I think, was at Bougival, early March 2014. We spoke of literature. We drank red wine in the buff on a big bed. I had shown off saying that we had "fucked," but he answered with a gentle smile from his long hair and three-day beard, with the look of somebody totally unimpressed by my free-spirited-woman escapades. "You could say we 'made love,' you know. That wouldn't mean that I would ask you to marry me or spend a family vacation in Corsica."

During those hours when I did not know if he had survived the Bataclan events, that's what I was thinking about. About that very joyful moment shared with him and the silence that then followed. I had written to him a few weeks later that I had met somebody, and he answered that we must be soul mates or something like that, because he had too. There was no embarrassment or cold spell, but I had then left Paris for the year, and there were no more book fairs to meet at. And the months went by, just like that, without the slightest second thought, until the night of Schrödinger. I told myself that Erwan couldn't die, as the dawn broke over the fields spread out before my window, because I had never told him thank you. My worry was purely and violently selfish. If I refused the possibility of his death it was not because of everything he would have left hanging, but because of what I would have not had the time to do.

At the beginning of fall 2013, the boy with whom I had been living for five years broke up with me out of the blue and left me in a mess on the floor of the apartment that bore signs of him everywhere and that I could not stand anymore. For months, I was convinced that I would never be able to touch a man, or be touched by a man again. I was certain that my body had been so perfectly made for his that any other skin, hand, mouth (and I'll spare you the digressions about genitalia that nevertheless crystallized the lion's share of my fear), would appear so radically foreign that no pleasant interaction would be possible. Due to this, I stopped going out. I wrote a lot. That helped me keep standing and not feel too miserable. I told myself that the rest of my life could flow on like that. And yet, January of the year after, I kissed Erwan in a kitchen, and we went to his place together.

We were drunk and giddy. I don't remember any more exactly how the night spun out. All I know is that the next morning's hangover was not able to chase away the pleasure I felt, because I had been awakened. That was what my whole body was murmuring.

I played through these thoughts over and over, swearing to myself that if Erwan was not dead, I would tell him about all the good he had done me. I would tell him as well that writing, that the friends who watched over me, that those many escapes to various forgotten corners of the French countryside had brought me back from that hell of sadness and apathy that I thought I would never climb out of. I made myself these beautiful promises up to the point when I learned that Erwan had been wounded, but was alive. From that moment on, I cried joyful tears, and then, smartly, shut my mouth. Because once I knew that he was alive, I wondered, all alone in the silence of my room, in that twilight sleep that makes any lame song of summer haunting and unimportant, I wanted to know, now that Erwan's life had been spared, what could be known, what he had been thinking about, while he was Schrödinger's cat, suspended between life and death for a few hours.

22

Facebook Status—11/28/2015

Exactly two weeks ago I arrived in this hospital, losing blood, paralyzed, frozen, ripped to pieces by pain. I wasn't able to do it discreetly. Blame it on an FB status where I expressed my happiness to go see EODM at the Bataclan.

I'll be leaving the hospital in a few hours to start my recovery at the family home. It would seem I won't have any after-effects. I can't do that discreetly either (or in my cowboy boots, because nobody can find them in the hospital!). Too many people were worried, because of that damnable FB status that I regret so.

Between those two points in time, I have only thought about myself, even more than usual. About healing. About dealing with my phobia of needles and getting my blood pressure taken. More generally, anything that more or less touches the field of medicine gives me a panic attack, or even makes me pass out. Yes, I know. We have a word for that: Sissy.

Between those two points in time, and above all else, I have been in contact with the most beautiful and noble part of humanity: compassion, devotion, listening, generosity, exchange, sharing, affection, sweetness, tenderness.

From the hospital staff, who have overwhelmed me with their daily altruism and good intentions, even in the smallest of their smiles.

From those closest to me, who have brought me so much strength and love that it became almost indecent to be so well surrounded by such people.

From you, right here, who I don't know at all or barely, who I have run into from time to time, or not, otherwise than on FB. You, right here, those virtual friends who have sent me such touching messages or comments of support. I fear that I have not been able to answer all of you individually. Please do forgive me.

With a thought filled with emotion for those who were not as lucky as I am, I just wanted to tell you this, truly, and apologies if you are allergic to soppy sentiment.

THANKS.

23

HERE WE WERE OUTSIDE OF THE WORLD.

Here was a nest, familiar smells, furniture that had survived all the moves, habits, umbrella pines and a view on the hills, olive trees, flowers to water when your parents aren't there.

Here was your father's cellar and your mother's good meals. Alas, you didn't know what filth they made you swallow for your own good at the hospital, but for four days, a nagging dysgeusia would make every sip taste like vinegar and every bite taste like slop. Without mentioning that you couldn't stay seated on your nonetheless comfy donut cushion for over five minutes without having the pain awake from your operated innards.

Here, we got things ready. You squatted your parents' room on the ground floor. Furniture and cables were arranged so you could work on your novel from bed. You also had to finish up government-aid files for the historical monument you were restoring. We took care of the nurses (one visit a day for the shots and to change the bandages), the personal trainer, the cushions, the elevated toilet seat. The ambulance trip from Créteil to the Gard region was awful. There was a stop-off at your place in the Poitou region to pick up some items. You stumbled into the full swing of the Christmas market. You ran into many acquaintances, whereas you, limping, disheveled, and wan, would have preferred more discretion. The end of the voyage was particularly terrible. You hurt, and your wound was infected, which wafted a foul odor throughout the ambulance that the sachets of lavender bought at the gas station could not hide. In the parking lot, you smoked your first cigarette in fifteen days, and it was good.

Here was a cocoon and love. Your parents hid their grief and worry at seeing their son so diminished. You didn't want anyone to feel sorry for you. Because you had nothing to be sorry about. This was not a posture, not just talk. You were very much aware of your luck. Lucky to have a loving, generous, and thoughtful partner. Lucky to have incredible parents, considerate friends, and a warm family. Lucky to be able to benefit from social security and an efficient public health system. And there were all those little gestures, that solidarity, those strangers who bent over backwards to help you at the pharmacy, at the public health agency at Poitiers, at the medical lab, at the insurance office. Human nobility, solidarity, and togetherness are really something else, when we let them blossom.

Here, everything was done to make your recovery comfortable. And yet, those first two nights, it was impossible to sleep. Not because of the (still striking) pain, not because of images of the events or memories. Just a deaf, insidious anxiety, that tied your gut in such knots to make you scream out of rage and powerlessness each time you turned off the lights. You decided to get a grip on that vise: hypnotherapy. You scrolled through the pages and sites of the town's specialists. One photo stopped you. Or rather one face. The impression of goodness and altruism. Marie-Christine would be the one. You would later learn that the day after the events of November 13 she had signed up on a list of practitioners ready to help victims pro bono. After a good hour-and-a-half session, half spent chatting, which is part of the therapy, your mental connections were softened, even bypassed by a modified state of consciousness. And you had some tools to use. Marie-Christine did not want you to pay her. You insisted, with the idea that an essential part of the healing process was that it would cost you something.

That very evening, you went to sleep easily and didn't wake until morning, because of the physical pain. When nerves grow back and get back into action, they let you know about it. With your infected wound, going to the toilet was even more painful. Your morale tended to match the state of your body: run down.

And above all else, you could not get a hard-on.

During those first days of December, that was your obsession, your main anxiety. You had always had joyful, upright boners, readily aroused and quickly operational. And a hardy sexuality. If you were to no longer get a hard-on … That was *unimaginable*. Seeing your poor, numb, puny penis in the shower, and no longer having an inkling of libido, made you panic. You knew that you had to be patient with your affliction, that the bullet's path had damaged that region. (Skimming through the hospital reports, you read: ballistic trauma with wound of the inner pudendal artery and arterial cavernous fistula, fracture of the right pubic ischium, cutaneous lesions from the buttocks area, bleeding at the level of the base of the penis, emphysema of the soft tissue of the hip and top of the thigh, grave lesions concerning the perineal artery, intravesical bubble and air bubble along the obteratur internus. Pseudoaneurysm with active bleeding of the pudendal artery.) Nevertheless, your worry remained resistant to all logical discourse. You were made of your experiences, your doubts, your ambitions, your family and social roots—and your manhood. You aspired to be recognized as a likeable individual, a respectable writer, and a noteworthy lover. You wished to draw no glory from this avowal, but when you saw in a partner's look that burst of gratitude from the female to the male who gave her bliss, you perceived vanity. Even if that was never what you were looking for in love-making, you would like to think. Becoming a man who can no longer get it up would be, you could feel it, a terrible lesson to learn.

No.

No. Impossible.

You asked Francesco about it in worried e-mails. He did not know. He was sorry. You had to be confident, be patient. The corrections of your novel, in which sexuality plays a major role, brought you back ceaselessly to your plight. You talked it over with your personal trainer, your doctor, your nurses, and even in your Facebook thread. You could accept, you'd sometimes say, still having a little limp, only ever being able to wear two-tone shirts and white socks, never eating chocolate again, in exchange for the return of your erectile performance.

Never be able to get a hard-on anymore? "I'd prefer death!" you would have exclaimed before. Now, you didn't know any more.

(A "work of literature," right? What a joker ...)

24

HYDROXYZINE **HYDROCHLORIDE**: treats minor anxiety.

Tramadol hydrochloride: analgesic belonging to the opiate family. "It acts on the central nervous system and relieves pain by acting on nerve cells, particularly those of the brain and spinal cord."

Chlorpromazine (the funniest one): antipsychotic. "It acts on the brain. It is used to treat illnesses characterized by symptoms such as hearing or seeing things that do not exist, having unusual suspicions, skewed beliefs, incoherent speech and behavior, and being emotionally and socially withdrawn. Individuals with this illness can also feel depressed, guilty, anxious, or stressed. Can provoke undesirable side effects, but not systematically in all subjects, such as: feelings of dizziness when you move quickly from a reclining or seated position to a standing one, dry mouth, difficulties urinating, constipation or even interruption of bowel movements (intestinal blockage), vision problems with impairment of your eyes' ability to see far away or up close (focusing problems), drowsiness, anxiety, mood swings, trembling, rigidity or abnormal motion, **impotency** or sexual frigidity, weight gain, interrupted periods, increased breast volume, abnormal lactation, changes in blood-sugar levels, changes in body temperature, venal blood clots particularly in the leg area (symptoms include swelling, pain, and redness in the leg area) that can travel through veins to the lungs and provoke chest pain and difficulty breathing. If you experience any of these symptoms, consult your physician immediately.

"The following side effects occur more rarely: cardiac rhythm problems (which can in exceptional cases put your life in danger), a skin allergy with a heightened skin reaction when you are exposed to sunlight or uv rays, liver illness with jaundice of the eyes and skin, fever, heavy perspiration, paleness, body muscle rigidity, consciousness impairment. If these signs appear, you must immediately stop the treatment and warn your physician or emergency medical team.

"The follow side effects occur exceptionally: an inflammatory illness targeting notably the skin (systemic lupus erythematosus), a marked drop in white blood cell count that can cause serious infections (agranulocytosis), brownish deposits in the eye that do not generally affect vision, and **painful and prolonged erections**."

You mistrusted drugs. Or rather, your body mistrusted them. With molecules and chemistry, you felt that we were lazily aiming to rip up everything rather than selectively pluck out creepers and weeds. This instinctual defiance had stopped you from ever dropping ecstasy or taking so-called hard drugs. You put trust in your ability to fight sickness, a faith that kept you down with the flu for several weeks more than once. You had ordered your organism to drive it out, but in vain. You now ordered it to give you erections, also in vain.

You had boxes of drugs next to your bed, piles of boxes, but you didn't take any of them. At first. Because it smarted so much that you very quickly had to take another look at your principled position. Staying seated was unbearable, you were in pain standing up, in pain lying down. You were in pain all the time. Nerve pain woke you up at night, to the point of screaming and chomping down on your pillow. So you tried various painkillers, identified the one that seemed the most effective and held onto it. Your doctor confirmed that you needed to take *all* of them, regularly, and not just when the pain hit. You remained bullheaded. A month later, your doctor advised you to slowly wean yourself off of your opiate, given its strength, and to progressively lower the doses over many weeks. You did it cold turkey.

You read and corrected the proofs of *Marguerite* ... You were putting yourself back together. You often thought: a miracle.

The marvel would occur during the night of December 22–23. That afternoon you had seen your osteopath. You still wonder today if there was any cause and effect relation. In the middle of a vaguely erotic dream, you drowsily awoke to a downy atmosphere of sexual excitation. Your hand made its way down your stomach. With a jolt, you were totally awake. Frenzied, you groped around for your night-stand light switch. Your eyes had to confirm what your fingers had felt. A seeming stiffness in your manhood. A pathetic, weak swelling, unfitting for penetration. You nevertheless wanted to bellow out your relief and praise Priapus. You masturbated. It was awful, painful, flabby. You were subjected to the most unpleasant ejaculation of your lifetime, with nerves like needles riddling your right flank. It hurt everywhere around your penis, testicles, and perineum. It was lacerating, it was wracking, but you had had a hard-on once again. Soft and not very long-lasting, but a hard-on once again. Hallelujah! In the morning, you sent a triumphant text to Jeanne. You didn't talk to your parents about it over breakfast.

From that epiphany on, your convalescence took a much jollier turn. The physical rehabilitation exercises with the personal trainer (PT) seemed easier. You insulted your reluctant foot less often. You felt like you were getting to know again a body that only did what it wanted to, even though you had still lost all control over it. After all, was your perineum in any worse state than that of a woman who has just given birth? No reason to whimper and whine over your lot in life.

One evening, and against your custom, you watched a film on the television. *Largo Winch*, with actor Tomer Sisley. As a souvenir of that dinner with your friend Karen, during which he joined you. He was then just an unknown actor trying to make it. You had wondered if it was possible for any human to be both so handsome and so magnetic. You resented him for it and made absolutely no effort to be good company. Stupid little fuck. On the screen, characters wanting to escape were shot in the back. You could feel the slugs that waylaid the fugitives burrowing into your own flesh. You told yourself that even if you could have a hard-on again, you would never be as you were before.

It was not your best Christmas, but it was definitely the most emotional. Not well enough to travel, you had to give up on celebrating New Year's Eve in Lyon, where many of your old pals were getting together. You nevertheless made an effort to dress up for the festive dinner prepared by your mother and father. Compassion glowed in their eyes when, after twenty minutes, demoralized and in tears, you went to put your sweat pants on. Wearing a normal pair of trousers hurt too much. Once back at the dinner table, your dad offered to go put on his pajamas for a laid-back celebration. Your mother reckoned that matching jogging pants and a white button-down shirt would make a real splash. You recognized how lucky you were to have such wonderful parents. Everything starts there, right?

As Seen from Outside: XII

MONDAY, NOVEMBER 16, 8:58 PM, TEXT TO ERWAN
Went back home without going boxing. Don't feel like
throwing punches. Don't feel like getting punched.
Don't feel like talking about it yet. Don't feel like being
felt sorry for. Nor held by anybody but you, Paule, and
the family. Just an urgent need for a little peace and
quiet. For love running like threads in the air, your hot
skin, your smile, and your impatience, my beautiful
love, that beautiful living face. My man against a pole—
in the 18th arrondissement, and the saving pole in that
fucking concert hall. My man against a pole. My love,
my Romeo, how scared I was, how happy I am.

Between 10 pm and 4 in the morning, while waiting
for news from Erwan, I was bombarded, naturally,
by thousands of thoughts. Those that needed to be
shared were shared with Bertrand. Hopes and terrors.
The one that never crossed my lips was the one that
would have created the scene of the "last time," "the
last words." It ate away at me all night long.
   We had spent Friday afternoon at my place. Each
working in our own room. I had to leave at 7 pm for
boxing practice, and Erwan a little later for his concert.
We had all afternoon to find the moment when we
could jump each other's bones. Offer ourselves a
naked moment, a bonding moment, an afternoon

delight. And that moment never came. We didn't take the time. I didn't find the time, or not at that moment when Erwan was looking for it. There was nothing to explain. It didn't seem serious. We were going to spend the weekend together anyway. We'd make up for it.

I finished putting my bag together. We talked about what to do after the concert. ("We'll meet up for dinner? With your pals?" "No, I'm going alone, Jeanne. Everybody turned down the invitation. They have a dinner together tonight. I'll just come back here afterward." And, "Are you going early to get a good seat?" "No need. I'm tall. I can see well even far from the stage. I prefer being at the back of the dance floor near the sound console. I'll get there during the opening act. No need to come too early.") It was looking as if the end of my practice and the end of the concert would coincide. We'd find each other at home in a few hours.

It was time for me to get to the gym. I was in the hallway getting ready to leave.

"Jeanne! We haven't fucked!"

I didn't turn around. I kept heading to the door.

"After boxing, Romeo. After boxing!"

After boxing, Romeo. After boxing.
After boxing, Romeo. After boxing.
After boxing, Romeo. After boxing.

After boxing, Romeo. After boxing.

We could have made love before boxing. Fucking damn it ...

Friends and acquaintances, Erwan's family and mine, used words to describe me like strong, organized, calm under pressure, and other praiseworthy terms for such circumstances. My cool reaction scared me, still scares me now, without making me hate myself too much. I know I had somewhat heroic thoughts. I don't hate myself. That's called shock, an escape hatch, a protection mechanism. But I do have a true feeling of remorse.

The next day. Saturday morning. It was maybe 11 am. I managed to get Erwan on the phone. It was the first time that I had heard his voice since his departure for the concert. I still had in mind our desire to make love "after boxing." I don't what first words we exchanged. I asked him to talk to me about his wounds. Erwan spoke only one sentence:

"I don't know if I'll ever get a hard-on again."

And I chuckled, "Stop. That's not funny!"

"No, no, Jeanne. It's serious. I don't know if I'll ever get a hard-on again."

I was left speechless out of shame for having giggled. I might have managed to get out an "Oh. Okay."

What a stupid bitch! What a stupid bitch! Your lover-escaped-alive-from-the-Bataclan talked to you, confided in you. You didn't know, had no idea what he was suffering through, enduring, thinking. How his body and mind were doing. And you? What did you do? You thought he was being a smart aleck. And you didn't even know how to immediately correct your faux-pas by saying "Sorry ..." A rotten little "Oh. Okay." Lame, Jeanne.

He asked me to bring his manuscript. And a red pen.

I don't know how the call ended. I felt pitiful. Disgraceful. Pathetic.

I got ready to rush over to see him at last in Créteil with Bertrand and Charlotte. I was thinking out all the ways I could apologize. I thought about nothing else for two hours. Formulated a thousand sentences, from the most elegant to the most forthright, to tell him just how wretched I felt.

But finding Erwan alive and conscious at the hospital swept away all other considerations. And even if I was thinking about my blunder, I couldn't manage to ask him for forgiveness. And I was angry at myself for it. And every day afterward, I would go to the hospital swearing I would ask him for forgiveness that day. And wouldn't do it. And didn't explain myself.

My lover's erection was certainly more than masculinity, virility, pleasure sex intimacy orgasms the pleasure of the other's pleasure. It was even more than our last exchange before the concert and our yearning to see each other again. The evolution of Erwan's erection, from the first morning of the first day at the hospital, was like a contract between my shame and myself. "If he can get a hard-on like before, I will be forgiven."

My TV was broken on November 13. I saw no live images. And very little afterward. Almost nothing. My universe of terror was limited to Erwan at the Bataclan.

The cafés, Jeanne. Don't forget the cafés.

I'd forgotten about the cafés because I couldn't see where it had happened and hadn't seen any images. I recognized none of the attacked bars and none of the victims.

Don't forget the Stade de France. But I had forgotten the cafés and the Stade de France.

Because it was only the Bataclan that counted. Because Erwan had escaped alive from the Bataclan. Only Erwan-escaped-alive-from-the-Bataclan existed. And after Erwan-escaped-alive-from-the-Bataclan, I didn't give a rat's ass about knowing whether or not my job had any meaning or whether or not I was doing my part as a busybody citizen of this One and Indivisible Republic.

There were so many deaths that I couldn't manage to say, "Erwan was at the Bataclan." I had to say, word for word, "Erwan escaped alive from the Bataclan." A magic formula.

The one time I said, to my neighbor, "My lover was at the Bataclan," he exclaimed, "Oh, Jeanne! All my sympathy!" No, no, no. Erwan escaped alive! From my neighbor's reaction, I thought for a fraction of a second that I had dreamed up Erwan's warm hand in mine at the hospital, and that I had abruptly been shaken from a repressed state of mourning.

25

ONCE UPON A TIME, there was a man who had never lived through anything traumatic. Who had never suffered. Never *really* suffered—we are not talking here about narcissistic wounds or day-to-day disappointments. Beings are woven out of their lost ones and their ghosts, wail for dead children or children who were never born, moan from cancers or from crushed limbs—from alcohol or not respecting the right of way. But this man, no. Let us call me the Writer. In his novels, he nevertheless strove to throw the world into question. To his mind, there was no need to have weathered violence or destiny. He held that he could quite easily send a character off to visit Peru without ever having himself set foot there. Or have a working-class, orphaned lesbian die of heartbreak. He, a middle-class straight man who never forgets to send a text message for Father's Day or a little book for his mother's birthday. He did not hesitate to create hired guns, rebels, and terrorists without ever having met one.

Lachesis, one of the Three Fates, disagreed intensely with this opinion, and so decided to put the Writer to the test. One Friday the 13th, she sent him into the heart of Chaos—according to Hesiod, the original chasm that preceded the creation of the world and all the gods.

Lachesis took care to send him there alone. All those who should or could have accompanied him that night were hampered by trickery of which only she knew the secret. Thus his befuddled friends would not buy their tickets in time, accepted other engagements, almost came at the last moment but then backed out. His partner, who would usually go to concerts with him, hesitated and then preferred to go to her kick-boxing practice. Two friends who had considered joining him, *Surprise!*, would not put their plan into action. Each thought that they had acted freely and properly. "What a stroke of luck!" they would exclaim here. "It's a miracle!" they would add there. Lachesis and her two sisters laughed.

A test, not a punishment. The Writer had to be wounded, but not excessively. No vital organs compromised, no mortal blow. Lachesis set him before a pole, to protect him from the first spray of bullets, then traced out the fateful bullet's trajectory. A few inches lower and his genitals would have been decimated. A few inches higher and his spinal column would have been shattered. A few inches more to the right and the femoral artery would have been sliced, leading him to a quick death from hemorrhaging. Lachesis set him before a post, traced out the trajectory of the bullet (wounded, but not excessively), raised the gunman's weapon, and aimed it in another direction. You're either one of the three Fates, or you're not.

What was the probability that the Writer, who did not live in Paris, would go to that concert? How many of the

1,500 spectators had been hit by at least one bullet? Out of the wounded spectators, how many would have no or barely any repercussions? One test. Not a punishment. One can recognize Lachesis's skillful hand here, don't you think?

A few inches difference … It's always a question of a few inches difference, right? Or seconds. Same thing. Call it the irony of fate, if that suits you. Lachesis and her sisters laugh. They have a good sense of humor. Or rather, you be the judge: Our man was hit in the butt, while but a few days earlier, his editor and he had chosen the title for his next novel, *Marguerite Doesn't Like Her Butt*.

Call it chance, if you wish.

There is no lack of terms, hailing from all cultures, to define those men and women that triumphant Western rationalism looks upon with, at best, circumspection, and, at worse, condescension and contempt. Mediums, fortune tellers, psychics, wizards, soothsayers, shamans … Is it conceivable that some people can perceive beyond their five senses and be more or less conscious, have more or less clear access, to that which remains sealed off to most of us? If we truly wish to turn everything into an equation, isn't it possible to link some of these phenomena to the theories of relativity?

Almost six thousand miles and seven time zones away from the Bataclan, the Writer's family waited for news, between anguish and despair. Except his father, who remained calm and composed. "I knew you were alive," he would tell him later. "I felt it deep inside of me."

A few months after the Test, our man saw Marie again, a radiant woman he had bumped into at a party two years before, but with whom he had immediately made a lovely connection.

"My God!" she cried. "Look at your aura … It's crazy!"

If the Writer was not unaware of what an aura was, he did not know that he possessed one (blue), and even less that his aura could make someone (a medium?) cry out in public. It would seem that it was already there two years earlier. It would seem that it had grown, intensified, and that it radiated outward a lot. And that the Test may not have been foreign to this positive transformation.

Anyway …

Chance, the irony of fate, or Lachesis doing her job. The doctors also had a job to do to get the Writer back on his feet, following methods owing nothing to magic or sorcery but to Science, that daughter of Reason. The cocky physical therapist Rémi took care of our non-hero during the first part of his convalescence. Exercises, massages, manipulations. It concerned making nerves, muscles, and tendons functional again. Medicine has taught us how all that is connected together. The same causes produce the same effects. How long past is the time of kindly blood-lettings and soothing enemas!

We were at the beginning of the month of December. It was a session like any other. Rémi was massaging the calf of the right leg. Suddenly, an electrical jolt shot through the Writer's leg up to the perineum. His whole body sizzled and went numb. Goose flesh. His breath halted. A lump formed in his chest and poured out a flood of tears and hiccups. Rémi continued with his massage. The freeing sobs would abate only after ten good minutes. The Writer told himself that tension was being evacuated. Not everything is hiding in the brain, or rather, everything is connected. We're not going to reinvent the wheel here.

Back home a few weeks later, he continued his convalescence in the hands of Justine. One morning, as the young PT was massaging his calf, the same scene repeated itself. Chills, numbness, tears. Justine was shaken up. She advised the Writer to consult Anne-Cécile, an osteopath who was not averse to working on the energies of the human body. Curious about different practices, different manipulations, different perspectives, our man made an appointment. He spoke to Anne-Cécile about both those emotional reactions happening three months apart following the treatment of two different PTs. She furrowed her brow. "Didn't you tell me that someone was holding onto your calf for hours at the Bataclan?" Had the energies of that wounded person who was desperately grasping the Writer's leg remained engraved in his flesh? Does the body have a memory that could stock up trauma too?

Well, all right …

New visit with Anne-Cécile, three months later. Before starting the session, she asked the Writer about his physical state. There was still the lack of sensation around the right foot area, right ankle still stiff, lack of sensation also around the perineum, the impression that the right buttock was separate from the rest of the body, as if dead weight. A fat, floppy pudding cake. The practitioner placed her hands on the ankle of her patient, reclining on his back, for many minutes, and then finished by sighing:

"I can't do it. It won't let me in."

"My ankle?"

"Your ankle. Your foot. The ways in are blocked."

Well, all right …

She shook her head, then started again, as if she had had a vision.

"Would you mind if we tried something?"

"Okay."

"Put yourself in the position you were in when the bullet entered."

"In the fetal position?"

"Yes."

She placed one hand on the Writer's right ankle and one on his left buttock. The Writer started to gasp and shudder. The fingers on his entry wound burned his skin. The burning sensation dug into his flesh. He was trembling inside as he let out long sobs. His left buttock was nothing but glowing lava. Over long minutes, he shook, he cried, he burned. Then, everything quieted down. Everything calmed down. He was under the physical impression of having rediscovered his normal butt. Anne-Cécile seemed as moved as he was. She stammered a little while explaining to him that …

"… your body had not understood that the bullet had

exited. So, I took it out. Anyway, I haven't finished. I'll finish up during our next session."

So, my Cartesian friends, any rational explanation?

At the beginning of the next PT session, Justine could not believe it.

"Your buttock has changed! It's incredible! There's no more bluish-yellow zone around the scar. And it doesn't have the same consistency to the touch. The tissue is less soft. I can feel muscles."

A rational explanation, sure, right?

"We're going to see how your body reacts around the scar left by the exiting bullet," Anne-Cécile offered, still just as amiable.

Very well then. The best way for nothing to happen is to expect something. So the Writer tried to stay circumspect. Very quickly, however, his body tensed up, reared up, jolted up. Tightened up. Folded up into the fetal position. He did not cry this time, but let out whimpers, whines, and sighs. It felt like he was in the middle of an exorcism. He rolled over on the table, shrunk up, stretched out. Uncontrollable. Nevertheless aware. Of his twisted face. Of his electrical body. As if forces foreign to his willpower had taken command of his muscles. Spasms. He arched up, then fell back down on the massage table. It would sometimes quiet down, and then Saint Vitus's dance would start up even stronger. To finally leave our man exhausted. From energies that were harmonizing, being liberated, being tuned.

"We went much further back than the Bataclan," Anne-Cécile said.

The same circus occurred during the next session, around the perineum this time. The Writer pressed on it with two fingers, then his palm, then with his fists, before taking his testicles and penis in hand. He rubbed them, rearing up and gleaming, almost obscene. Untamable drives. It went on like that for twenty, maybe forty minutes. "You have taken control," Anne-Cécile told him. He felt once more as if he had suffered. But the result was the return of a semblance of sensation of that part of him that had been banished in the vortex of it all.

Who believes that a body can accumulate the energy from another body and return it in tears? That flesh can be persuaded that a bullet is still lurking within when it had only passed through in a fraction of a second, ten months before? Who believes that three immortal sisters, called the Moira in Greek mythology and the Fates by us, spin, measure, and cut the threads of our existences? And if the Writer had been put to the test—come on, let's admit it, let's not be narrow-minded—let's say by Fate—then why? To what end?

You know nothing about it. All faith is a choice. It is not out of the question, however, that the end of this story may bring us an answer (works of literature and cliffhangers are not incompatible).

As Seen from Outside: XIII

How could anyone fall for that stupid belief that
nothing, absolutely nothing, could ever happen to him
as long as I, his father, was alive? How could anyone
live with that belief, and many others too, that are
just the fruit of a much-assuring imagination, because
it creates a protective shield? A smokescreen that
masks, that fools, that definitively holds each one of us
in our roles.

You have always been part of my life without you
realizing it. A victim as much as I am of that kind of
hierarchy that insidiously moves in and then sets itself
up. Weird, right? Because, first of all, why would anyone
want to flip roles, then doubt that you, my son, could
not lead your promising destiny to its fruition? We all
have a bit of road to travel. Yours, although already
full of beautiful experiences, has only just begun, and
great fortune waits on your horizon. While me, let's be
realistic, I am not very far from closing up shop!

Erwan will go through those inevitable obstacles
with his head high, and nothing will weigh him down.
It's etched in stone. That's how I was wired, but it was
above all how I experienced the beginning of your, of
our, ordeal.

Why do I have this wonderful assurance? That
question may seem completely out of place when
it comes to what you lived through. But asking it,

and above all answering it, is a way to explain my experience on that morning of November 14, when I learned in Hanoi that you might be among the victims. It is also probably like therapy, given the terrible feeling I have of being so completely out of sync with the anguish of your mother, your brother, and his wife Hien. For too many long hours, we had had no news, but I had no doubts. Because a very long time again a fortune teller in a shadowy back kitchen had told me that I shouldn't be worried, "Your sons are in good hands. They will succeed." She even added that the eldest would be famous! Given that fame had not yet arrived, I stupidly deducted—this was my analysis—that you could only be alive on that November 14. It so happened that you were very lucky. It wasn't your time. That's what I realized on the 16th, when I saw you lying on your hospital bed. That was a brutal shock.

Since that day, many cracks have undermined the foundations of my inner self, and all sorts of uncertainty has gnawed away at the base of that construction I have been building for years.

Is evil an endemic reality for mankind? What mechanism can activate such waves of violence? Are we constrained to accept these assaults without having to explain them, other than by acknowledging the right to be different, the right to strike back, the right to suffer the restrictions of our hard-won freedoms year after year? Do we all come from the same atoms? Are we all the offspring of Adam, what some would call the "children of God," destined to watch our own brothers and sisters murder each other and keep on surviving without trying to understand what is wrong with the world?

Faced with the absurdity of current discourse, condescending to victims and their loved ones, wanting above all else to pull away from extreme reactions and not fall into the endless cycle of hatred and the desire for vengeance, I truly started to doubt. That is to say, confronted with these almost-daily scenes of barbary, I began to ask myself where we really come from and where we were going.

The latest answer I have found to this question, and there wasn't much room for chance, came to me while reading a book on the Four Horsemen of the Apocalypse. Strangely, what had seemed completely absurd from my adolescence on suddenly took on a new light.

Apocalypse is a word that is often used to describe the excessive nature of a catastrophe, a misfortune. It is actually synonymous with the "end of the world."

The Apocalypse of Saint John, so the end of the world, closes the New Testament and relates to

Genesis, which at the beginning of the Old Testament describes the creation of the world. *Apocalypse* comes from the so-called Late Greek *apokalupsis*, which translates as "revelation, unveiling," and from the verb *apokaluptein*, which means "to translate, to reveal."

There is surely a cycle that, in an esoteric and highly symbolic manner, recounts the history of our Earth, and of our day-to-day life upon it. How can we decipher these writings that are parts of sacred texts that have been the source of meditation and interrogation for millennia? And above all, how can we not see the current context as a warning signal?

Those four horsemen, whose number brings us back to the four cardinal directions, ride horses that are white (the first), fiery red (the second), black (the third), and pale (the fourth). It has been said, and then I will wrap up this reference, that "power was given unto them over the fourth part of the Earth, to kill with sword, with hunger, with death, and with the beasts of the Earth."

I hope that is all just another nightmare, and that tomorrow I will wake up under peaceful skies, telling myself, Erwan, that we still have many things to say to each other and many good times to share.

26

YOU WENT BACK HOME IN MID-JANUARY, 2016. On your own two feet. You made a stopover in Paris and organized an aperitif with Jeanne in a bar to see your friends again, come one, come all, no obligation, no RSVP. As if everybody had needed such a moment, with reunions and joyful company, chasing away fears. The bar quickly became too small. We kissed each other. We cried. We hung out. We even worked things out. How pointless old clashes suddenly seemed! You knew that their love had changed the bullet's direction as much as the schemes of Lachesis. They might even be linked …

You went back home more obsessed than ever by the future of your erections—short and painful. You got your hair cut, shorter than it had been for at least ten years. You were impatient that *Marguerite* … would hit the bookshelves.

You went back home thin, it would seem, and certainly not very hardy. Still forced to sit on a donut cushion, electrical tingles in your foot, and three PT sessions a week. Sensitivity had not completely returned to your right leg. Your muscles were atrophied. Your slightly jammed ankle made your walk a little wobbly. And blast it all, your hard-ons were soft! Tell me that it's going to come back, please, I beg of you! Tell me my penis is not going to keep this weird shape, a little dented, twisted, strangely red. That it won't stay so cold, like your extremities in winter. Cold, as if life had been sucked out of it. Cold, like a life sentence.

You went back home, and the mayor of the village ran into you on the street one morning. He shook your hand for a long time and asked you for your news. You learned that on the day of national commemoration, he had talked about you in his speech. For two years, you had been restoring a historical monument three hundred yards from the town hall. When you asked for financial support from the municipality to renovate the façades, they replied—in the negative—only after three reminders on your part. When you asked the town council to come visit the site, they ignored you the first time, then stood you up the second. When you opened the doors of the monument for European Heritage Days, the mayor did not stop by. They didn't give a hoot about a novelist rehabilitating a fifteenth-century building. But a Bataclan survivor who lives in his commune, now that, on the other hand, piqued the mayor's interest. At the café and the marketplace, the faces were supportive and compassionate. Modest restraint coated greetings.

You went back home, and the world continued its upward march. One status replaced another on the screen. Terror hit Brussels. A part of Europe was flooded. Orlando was in mourning. The Euros soccer tournament made all the headlines. Amazement had replaced dread. "You were at the Bataclan, really?" You were exotic, and not pitiful any more. Azzaro had created a perfume in a barrel-shaped bottle, "elegant and bold," according to their ads. "The perfume for the man for whom anything is possible. An alluring, brazen hero, that men envy and women desire, tries his luck." People minded their tongues in front of you. They went "Whoops!" and said they were sorry when they thought they had blundered by using such expressions as "What a pain in the ass," "What a sex bomb," or "That blew me away." Relax, my friends. I am alive and not made of china. People used kid gloves to broach the subject. They didn't dare to. They beat around the bush. They bit their tongues. But talking about it did not upset you. Others forbid themselves from bringing up their own misfortune or hard times, or even their troubles. "Given what you've been through, it's nothing." You would swipe away that hierarchy of pain with a brush of your hand. "Let me love you, okay?"

The world continued its upward march. Scruples still stifled a minimum. You've got to make a living …

"Hello, yes. Good evening. Ummm. I am x, chief editor of [local big media]. I am calling because, uh, well, I know you were wounded at the Bataclan on November 13th. And, uh, you had refused to talk to us about it. But, uh … I was wondering … Would you accept to … now … discuss … the Brussels attacks?"

"On April 14th, my fifth novel will be in the bookstores. From there I would like to speak to you."

"Oh … uh … fine, too bad. Thank you. Goodbye."

The world marched on, unaware of your shame. Ashamed of your bony legs and your sagging buttocks. Ashamed of your too-flaccid penis. Your naked body was humiliating. You showed it, nevertheless. As a challenge? Because it was out of the question to lose that battle? Because you were going to have to accept yourself as imperfect, if ever everything remained in such a pitiful state? Your sexuality over the first months was a torture for you, much more mentally than physically. Having to accept that you could only barely penetrate, that your desire could not grow firm. Having to accept the unerotic nature of your wan, flabby flesh. Your faltering ego was put to the test.

You went back home, and the world marched ever upward. You could barely get it up. You consulted your general practitioner to check the scarring along the furrow between your buttocks and bring up your sexual anxiety with him.

"I have a young intern in the office right now, Mr. Lahrer. Would it bother you if she took part in our appointment?"

It would seem that a pretty girl had to be a witness to every embarrassing situation of my existence. (Thanks, Lachesis?) You accepted and, stronger than shame, proceeded to undress in front of this handsome fellow and the young woman. He described to her what had happened to your butt crack, which he spread wide to clearly show Francesco's repairs. Very nice work! You held back a nervous laugh. Everything was back in order, according to the physician, who asked you if you had also noticed the improvement.

"I never look at it."

"You don't look at it?" Handsome Fellow boomed. "Do you touch it?"

You wondered out loud, "How many people focus daily on their butts?" That had never crossed your mind. The young intern chuckled. Handsome Fellow encouraged you to touch and massage your scars. "You have to accept them and tame them." You recoiled at the thought (sissy), all the while aware that he was right. So, you started to talk to them in the shower. "You're part of the project, girls," you repeated to them every day. A project to reconstruct yourself. A project to get your physical integrity back. A project to get a strong hard-on again. Project B.

Handsome Fellow gave you permission to go regularly to the cardio-fitness gym next door. You lifted weights and did push-ups. You sweated it out on bikes and rowing machines. You reinvested your body at 170 beats a minute. Justine noticed the change under her caring fingers. She confirmed that you had gained muscle. Your ass was less "disfigured," as you sometimes joked.

"Aren't you angry at the terrorists?" your twenty-year-old cousin asked. No. You were angry at Julia, who betrayed you long ago. You were angry at François Hollande, who lied to his electors. You were angry at society, at the organization of the world, at economic oppression and intellectual misery. But not more than before. You weren't angry at anybody for that erection-hindering bullet. You did not know who your attackers were. You didn't know their names. They did not exist. Because if it hadn't been them, it would have been others. And others will come. The very incarnation of our failure to live together, scraps of the simulacra of our consumerist hedonism. Others will come. Famished, feeble-minded, narcissistic orphans of a world without bearings where everyone follows their own law, where a TV ad is called a "break." The rejected rubbish of ever-deeper inequalities. Others will come. They are already here. Off camera. Extras or silhouettes cut out during editing. Stuffed with injustice to the point of obesity. We would rather turn away, if we do not see them … They don't exist.

You stuck to thinking that our true inclination is to help each other out, to love each other always. When they put us into competition for jobs, grades, fastest times, sexual partners, we interiorize the struggle. The other becomes an adversary. When we instill fear and mistrust, the other becomes an enemy. Emergency, despair, and danger short-circuit those ultra-liberal inputs, those values that they want us to think are natural, and generosity and solidarity gain ground. You didn't know much about the thinking of Jean-Jacques Rousseau, but that guy has been mocked for centuries with his noble savage. We'd rather have the cynical, mean, virulent, caustic, mocking Voltaire than him. Is that so amazing?

You stuck to thinking that happy people don't kill anybody.

That age-old wisdom. He who sows the wind reaps the whirlwind. War had hit home. Mass murderers were among us. So, who did the sowing? And why?

The Bataclan: a symptom of a rotting civilization. An eruption of fear in the midst of a false pretense for a party. Elsewhere, in Tel Aviv or Islamabad, in Mosul or Abuja, it crisscrosses daily life. Here, we had been spared that danger. And all the better. Fighting, striking, face-to-face combat, killing, these are things we do not know anymore. Your generation had never known that. Never learned. And all the better? Without it, you were powerless when faced with the ultimate nihilism of someone who is ready to die, who has reached his final point of indignation where anything is better than what he has endured and suffered. He had been held at a distance, so he invited himself to join in the dance. And there was nothing we could do when faced with someone with nothing left to lose but their life.

So, what are we to do? Some write books, opinion columns, appeals. They weren't there. Their bodies know nothing. Which certainly should not stop them from giving their opinions. Or stop novelists from transforming current events into literary awards. Having taken a bullet does not give you more legitimacy to open your mouth, or more clearness of vision. We get worked up on social media, that creepy bog of rabid beasts that believe the fact they breathe gives them the right to belch out baseless opinions; that swarming cesspool of the ignorant, the jealous, and the quarrelsome; that heap of aggressive, anonymous, anonymously aggressive little navel-gazers, avatars unable to look past the horny tip of their "Me, myself, and I." We argue about more security, the state of emergency, the struggle against laxity, face buts, hear the sound of army boots and insults, watch Godwin's Law in action. That's what they are looking for. Somebody with a strategy. At least that's what you thought. You couldn't believe that it was all for nothing. That there would be nothing behind the pain, the frustration, the desire to exist. No. They want: to rip civil society to pieces. They want: hate. They want: communities to withdraw into themselves. They want: to make all of us fight each other.

Mistrust. Look over your shoulder. Reinforce the instinct for property. Reclaim our origins. Hands off my roots. Conspiracy theorists on the Web. Deniers. "Who has proven to us that …?" "And don't you find it weird that …?" "Just by chance …"

Unrestricted gun sales. International commerce, my good man. Dassault needs enemies. And what if we sent those hawks to the battlefields? To the front lines? So they might know what they're talking about. And what if we bombed their vacation homes and their posh neighborhoods, so they would know what it means to cower in a cellar? And what if we planted land mines in their gardens? Do you think it's normal that a weapons dealer owns a big daily newspaper? Is nobody bothered by that? You, ma'am, in the back to the right? No? Well then, next question. Secular culture. Outward signs of religious affiliation. France, Eldest Daughter of the Church. Burqa. Cross. Yarmulke. Public space. Is it being explained at school? In businesses? In the media? A citizen must be educated. But we haven't the means, good sir. Too many employer taxes, and then there's the debt ... Next question. Let's talk about cops assaulted on the street. Too few cops, not enough training. Is nobody bothered by that? We just told you that we don't have the means. Too many civil servants. And then there's the social security debt hole (*sic*). Next question.

So, what are we going to do? Explosions. Assassinations. Commemorations. Indignation. The human spirit reacts. Everybody was *Charlie*, but schizophrenic. After too many nights standing up in support, you sit back down exhausted. We vote for professionals who don't even need to be recycled because the ultra-present washes everything bright white. We trust the system that has created our hardship. Walk with your head down. Don't make eye contact. And that man over there, hanging out against the wall at Barbès, across from my friend Guillaume's place, what if he were to get the idea to go blow up the school next door?

It is possible. Terrorists have struck.

So, what are we going to do?

You get used to it. Soldiers in the train stations and in the streets. (Every time you run into them, you want to ask them if they have ever shot someone, if they have ever taken a bullet.) You get used to it, or you will get used it.

Bag searches. Frisking. We remind you that all luggage must be tagged. You get used to it. All abandoned or suspect baggage. You don't hear it anymore. It's for our own good, right?

One morning, you arrived at the building that housed the television station where you had been freelancing for ten years, in an easygoing mood. As usual, you swiped your badge on the sensor to open the entrance door. In the lobby, on top of the regular receptionist and security guard, was a new guard wearing a bulletproof vest. He demanded to see your badge and, suspicious, compared the photo printed on it to your face. The station had been acquired by an American group.

You get used to it.

Reminder: The goal of terrorism is to instill terror. And it works.

"Even me, right in the heart of the Poitou countryside, I think about it," your adorable personal trainer confessed to you. "So, I understand you being a little paranoid."

Paranoid?

Parking your motorcycle next to a catering truck and seeing it blow up.

Noticing a bearded Arab (you hated yourself) in a jogging suit and bomber jacket carrying a sports bag and hiding yourself out of firing range, behind a concrete pillar at the Montparnasse train station.

Seeing a big black man (you hated yourself) in the high-speed train rummaging through his suitcase for a good five minutes. Keeping your eyes on his moves in case he might have been trying to put together a disassembled weapon hidden in his things.

Sighting a haggard, Middle Eastern man with a moustache (you hated yourself) sitting a few seats down who wouldn't stop getting up to go to the toilet. Noticing he went back when the ticket inspector gave him a fine. (Well, he didn't have a ticket; what a surprise. You hated yourself.) Waiting for him to take out a weapon to waste the aforementioned inspector. Seeing that person's head quite clearly splattered against the sliding door. Taking a deep breath.

Paranoid?

The goal of terrorism is to instill terror. Your reality was modified by this possibility, of which your flesh carries the scars. "You're probably going to think this is silly," your ever-so-devoted personal trainer began, blushing with downcast eyes. "Don't make fun of me, okay, but each time I see the progress you're making, I tell myself that I'm fighting Isis and Co. too. That's my challenge. As if by putting you back together, I'm shouting to them that they're not going to win."

You wanted to hold her in your arms. Your eyes welled up with tears, but …

… Are they not going to win?

So, a dark-skinned guy (you hated yourself) sat down in the train's empty compartment, on the other side of the aisle. He was wearing a thick jacket that could have been hiding a belt of explosives. He was nervously fiddling with his cell phone, which was, *Good Lord!*, wired to a metal tube. He seemed lost and elsewhere, huddled up against the window. You told yourself you absolutely had to talk to him, so that some human contact would stop him for blowing up the train.

"Excuse me ... Uh ... Did you hear how long we'll be stopping at Valence?" you stuttered.

(Dark look.)

"It's just to know if ... Uh ... If I'll have the time to have a smoke."

"No, I didn't hear. I can look on my cell if you want."

"No! No, no, don't touch your ... I mean ... It's okay, I'll see ..."

The train stopped. The guy looked at you with insistence. Oh yeah, had to smoke a cigarette. You stepped out to the platform and lit up your smoke. The suspect joined you on the platform. He still seemed just as fragile, yet less threatening. He took the metal tube out of his pocket and started vaping. You would have burst out in laughter if you hadn't thought yourself so ridiculous.

Are they not going to win? You went to Paris less. Trains and train stations made you anxious.

A lot of luggage was placed in the middle of the train car, in the space set aside for that. Underneath was a small, pink, Hello Kitty bag. All of a sudden you wondered: If a Kalashnikov bullet were to shoot through it, would you have to get ready to protect the little girl that it belonged to?

The goal of terrorism is to instill terror. In that bar in the 10th arrondissement you often hung out in, your lover and you, there were big bay windows that you would see shatter from gunfire from time to time. You knew that you would not have the time to leap to cover her on the floor and use your body as a shield. But you got yourself mentally ready. You thought, nevertheless, that the presence of a nearby mosque said to be Salafist would protect you (you hated yourself).

Are they not going to win? One day, you were trying on various articles in the basement of that masculine underwear temple found in the Marais district. You suddenly thought that the store would be a good target for those morons who find homosexuality to be unnatural. You looked around to find the emergency exits. Images of salespeople lying bloody in the middle of tipped-over clothes racks seized you. You refused to give into panic and continued trying on the underwear. You bought a pair of boxers. Just because your hard-ons were going to be limp from now on didn't mean you couldn't be elegant.

Not even scared! You had seen that slogan on a poster for a post-Bataclan get-together. But you *were* scared. In your flesh and in your nerves. The law of the survival of the fittest is efficient. The history of humanity proves it every time. That's why it's harder (because less *natural*) to be on the left than on the right. Q.E.D.

"Do you have any psychological after-effects?"

"I wonder if I'll have a normal hard-on one day."

"Anything besides that?"

Besides that? *Besides that?* How do you want me

to drop "that"? There was nothing besides that? You noticed some improvements, sure, and you were able to have a satisfying sex life again. In ten months, you had got back 70 percent of your former capacities. You had fewer strange sensations during ejaculation, less pain afterward, and more sensitivity in the genital area. You sometimes felt petty to wallow in self-pity about your feeble phallus. Isn't it indecent to bring up your erection problems when you think about the number of dead, the severely wounded?

You didn't have the survivor syndrome, didn't feel any guilt over those who didn't make it. A terrible, deep, violent empathy, yes. They were your friends, your brothers and sisters. From time to time, you would read a portrait on the touching memorial that lemonade.fr had devoted to them. You wondered which photo they would have chosen for yours. Alone, in front of the screen, you communed with their loved ones, because you were one of their loved ones. You would sometimes click on a photo and speak to the person. Just a few words. I hadn't forgotten you. Without feeling guilty for being alive. None of the dead were angry with you for being alive. You knew that. They were living a bit through you. It was strange. A subtle throbbing. You never told yourself that you could have died. Even if you had believed that you were going to die. Some of your friends and family had thought you were dead. You were a survivor for them. Risen from the dead. They had gone further than you had in their torment. In a way, they had suffered more than you had.

You sometimes felt really lame for not feeling bad. You were a truly poor victim. At the Wine and Book Fair at Saumur, Agnès was talking to me about the rubber band theory, which would stretch out without you knowing it and then, one day, *slap!*, right back in your face. Yes, it's possible. But what does that mean? You weren't going to pretend to feel bad, right? In April, you were invited to a book fair in Bordeaux by your bookseller friend Rodolphe. Who had had a heart attack a few weeks earlier. Who had lost cartoonist friends in the *Charlie Hebdo* attack. At the restaurant on the last night, around a merry table, your jokes about the Bataclan and cardiac arrest went from bad to worse, which made you howl in laughter. The guests at the next table were shocked and outraged. (It's true that you were going really far.) When one of your friends informed them that both of you had been through the calamities that were making you laugh to tears, you saw their faces don the purest kind of bewilderment, the essence of incomprehension.

Live (continue to).

Laura and Ramez could not grasp it. That couple of friends had also been at the Bataclan, on the dance floor. You hadn't known that. If you had known, or if you had run into them in the concert hall, would you have followed them to the bottom of the stage? (Answer, Lachesis!) They survived, untouched, in the middle of the corpses and the dying, bathed in blood. Eight months later, they were still eaten up with guilt (Ramez is a doctor, which did not help matters), haunted by what they had seen, heard, smelled. They were supposed to meet us on Poopy's terrace to watch the Bastille Day fireworks shot off from the Trocadero and the Eiffel Tower. They sent a message early in the evening. Barely out of their home, the sound of firecrackers in the street had given them panic attacks. They made a U-turn. A few hours later, around a forgotten barbecue platter, nobody wanted to revel in the show that had just ended.

Nice. Fuck it. Nice.

27

NORMAL. *BANG!* Abnormal.
A little bit to the right: a survivor. One more step to the left: a victim. Dead.

Calm/Storm. Ejected out of the day-to-day. Submerged—but in what? Before/After. One second. A fraction of. Here/There. Choice. Something held me up. I am here. I am not there. *BANG!* What is that about? Luck? What impact? Calm/Tragedy. So close. Seen from below. Because seen from above, whatever. Dust. Write a book about dust? About that Being-Dust swept sooner or later under the rug of memory? Here or there. Calm/ Storm. Ordinary/Extraordinary. Unthinkable. War. *BANG!* The Sixth Extinction. The Regular, The Day-to-Day, Known Reality. *BANG! BANG! BANG!* Fresh look. Fresh bodies. Fresh focus(es). Black? Shift (No shift). Upper angle shot. As seen from above? Ask the dust. Not much to make novel out of, right, guy?

One thing is certain: It happened. Did it happen? You had written scenes without verve. Orphan syllables of sensation. Recreation. Groping about. No sinew. Enough to ask yourself if you were really at the Bataclan. And yet, that night, while you were doing the exercises that you had made up to tense and relax your glutes and perineum, you could almost see that bullet, the trajectory of that bullet. Iblis standing next to you. The scene shot from above. From outside. Almost. Everything went blurry soon enough. Zoom back. And then nothing. Dust. The sorrow of the families. You tried. You concentrated. You were at that concert. Firecrackers blast. Then nothing. Strings of perceptions. Intangibles. Where you at the Bataclan, that night? You had sometimes been of the mind that you had not seen such-and-such a film. Then a friend would tell you that they had seen it with you. Good one. If you had seen it, you would have certainly known that. Nothing would spring to mind. You are a duck's oily feathers, that let the real slide off them—so as to better create what comes next, perhaps? You even had doubts about your wound. You have never seen it. Francesco wanted to show you the photos that he had taken of your backside before operating on you. Never in your life, you had told him. Never, Francesco, do you hear me? Everyone was amazed that you hadn't taken a look at your scars in a mirror. They're behind me, don't you get it? When it happened, it was already behind me.

It happened. We can confirm that today. But what about in fifty or a hundred years? Or in three hundred years? There may be nothing left but a place-name stuck onto a date, somewhere in the archives. We will have forgotten the victims and the heroes of that horrible evening, just as we have forgotten the names of the soldiers killed in the absurdity of battle. At Auschwitz, the explanations and presentations of young guides sometimes contradict those of the survivors, who tell their accounts alongside the visits. The guides disagree with the survivors. If they were there, they could not have seen everything. Or they cast a doubt on the reliability of those old peoples' memory. Soon, there will be no more survivors. So of course, there wasn't much material to make a novel about your presence at the Bataclan. But to write was a gesture that proved that you might go on. A small gesture. And that term would again be appropriated to define your sort-of, so-egocentric work of literature. Not because "the people have the right to know," but because History must not forget. Literature does not stop bullets. Henri Barbusse, Louis-Ferdinand Céline, Erich Maria Remarque, Louis Guilloux did not stop World War II by writing novels about World War I. Henri Alleg did not stop Guantanamo. Anne Frank, Primo Levi, Henri Vercors, Georges Hyvernaud did not stop any genocide, any battle, any civilian massacre. Today, we still send kids off to get killed. Women are raped by the victors. Bastards feed the desire for vengeance. Literature does not stop bullets. On the other hand, it can stop a finger from pressing a trigger. Maybe. It's a bet worth making.

A work of literature ... Doesn't the phrase hide the will to master this project? Which would not serve it. Which would explain why you floundered about so much. You second-guessed and held yourself back. Why not a simple tale, as if you were just talking to your friends?

You balked. You fought against this feeling that you were writing for others. You were not even having any fun with this damned Project B.

Most likely, the first watershed moment was when you accepted to publicly describe the Bataclan. Banking off a side shot, in the guise of a writer and not a victim. For *Le Monde des livres*. Because the "Story of a Book" column was fitting, because you had revised and corrected and revised and changed and revised *Marguerite Doesn't Like Her Butt* during your hospital stay, and then during your convalescence. Because you were familiar with the journalist, and appreciated her kindness and compassion. Because she had an unbeatable argument: At the end of the novel, you acknowledged all the people who took care of you at the Henri-Mondor hospital, so what happened to you is not a secret. And to be perfectly honest, could you have refused the offer of an article about your novel in *Le Monde*? You were no less a saint than a hero.

When you read the article for the first time, in its digital version, you panicked. You should not have said yes. You were angry with yourself. You thought you were sensationalist, whore-mongering. Manuel was one of the first to react. "It was good to have done it like that," your Papa Bear wrote you. You were almost relieved to learn that a strike was planned for the very day the article would go out, stopping the daily papers from hitting the stalls. And then almost relieved to learn that the "Books" supplement in *Le Monde* would go out the next day instead. You were no less a saint than a hero.

Then you started talking about your Project B with your inner circle. With your author friends. They shared their enthusiasm with you. A beautiful enthusiasm. Which did not just warm your heart, but gave you a kind of legitimacy. You remember one night, at the Comédie du Livre at Montpellier, where Jérôme, Tatiana, and Olivier encouraged you over a few drinks. Jérôme, whose work you admired, even offered to give it a look, if needed.

A work of literature. Which filled itself out as it hobbled along. Arduously. It was difficult and unsatisfying. You paced around it. Good Lord, find the angle of attack! Because spewing out your little pangs and pains was out of the question. What an idea to have opened your mouth and announced that you were going to write that Project B! You felt the pressure. You felt something expected of you. And how far could you take it? You weren't alone in this story, which did not end well for everybody. The angle could not just be that of the individual within the crowd. So you jotted down ideas about chapters, and snippets like …

If we pan in, what can we see? Erwan is lying down on his bed. He is smiling. Tubes are sticking out of him all over the place. He is wearing a hospital smock. He does not seem defeated. Is he hamming it up for the camera?

… that you would not keep.

You had thought about writing in the third person, to put some distance between the events and yourself, but you found it silly to tell a tale whose hero was called Erwan, and even sillier to find another first name. So you were floundering about in the first person with your mediocre work of non-literature, when you decided to try out the second person, as when you try to shine up a grimy old wall. You were behind the wheel of your car rolling to Vierzon, where Juliette was bringing together some other friends at her place for a festive weekend. As you were passively letting your thoughts spin out around your work, France Culture radio was broadcasting the voices of Camille de Toledo, Alicha Imhoff, and Kantuta Quiros. What they were saying delighted you. Their words blended with your thoughts. You listened without understanding, and understood nonetheless. Your body understood. Your skull understood. That very evening, Marie, the one who sees auras, ended up opening the door with a few words. During your conversation, you clearly saw yourself spread out on the floor of the Bataclan, bearing it all and mastering nothing, in total lack of control (your nightmare). And then faced with the blank sheet trying to take control through writing with the vain ambition to create a "work of literature." Crushed by that responsibility. By the irreducible nature of what had happened.

So there you have it. It was time to become "I" again.

28

EVERYTHING WAS READY. Gourmet cocoa for the hot chocolate. Little pastries. Apartment tidy and clean. Anxiousness and excitement made acid course through my solar plexus.

Nathalie would be arriving soon.

I was madly in love with her. Messed up in love. A love at the edge of eighteen. Clumsy and stupid. Romanced. In love with being in love. Enough in love to write her poems—fifteen of them, even.

"I'm coming to town on Saturday. I'll stop by for a hot chocolate," she had said. Or, "I'll stop by at snack time." Or stop by for tea. At any rate, it was only the "I'll stop by" that interested me. Had she given a fixed time or mentioned late afternoon? I don't know anymore. She had some shopping to do, and then she would come. My studio apartment had been spit-and-polish since the morning. I had started to scour at dawn. I had skipped football practice. Now I was waiting, feverishly. The cocoa would be mixed with a bit of sugar, then you slowly add cold milk while stirring, until you obtain a creamy paste. Then you delicately blend the hot milk while mixing with suave strokes of a wooden spoon. Then you put it all in a pot over a very, very low flame. This beverage must be prepared at the last minute.

I waited.

Seated at the window, a big window that gave onto Rue du Bon-Pasteur, I waited. I had a view on both ends of the narrow street. I was going to glimpse Nathalie arriving by foot, or see her white Golf drive by with its windshield wipers, under which I had once or twice slide little messages that had gone unanswered. She always acted as if they had never existed. Have a hot chocolate. Or tea. Share a snack. I had bought pastries. Tidied the apartment. I was ready. Were we going to kiss? You couldn't consider Nathalie my girlfriend. It was more complicated. She was complicated. Dodging the subject. A subject I never dared broach directly. I'm the kind of guy who leaves messages under windshield wipers and writes poems. But she had said she was going to have a snack. At four o'clock. At late afternoon. Her shopping had most likely taken more time than planned. If only I was sure of myself. If only I had had her phone number. But cell phones didn't exist then. The Internet didn't either. We set up dates in person. To have a hot chocolate, for example. Or tea. And if you had to cancel, you'd call on the land line. Except if she was in town. That meant finding a telephone booth. And she would have had to buy a telephone card. Nathalie's phone number was the same as her parents, who she lived with. She knew my address. She was on her way. I would soon enough get the hot chocolate ready, and we would have our snack. Then we would kiss on the mattress on the floor, that was covered with a blanket and made do as a couch. To kiss her chocolate lips. That would be sweet. Perfect. Ideal. Or I would kiss her as soon as the door opened, with such an undeniable love throbbing between us. No, I wouldn't dare. I was not sure of myself. I was eighteen. I didn't know anything about love or women. Only what I'd read or seen in movies. And invented in the films and books I had authored. Soon to be famous. You'll see. I had theories about the subject, of course. Mystical. The fusion of body and soul. No need to talk to each other. Shared proof. In the real world, my theories would squeak and jam. For a long time, I would try to pressure the real to adapt to my ideals. The real always won. Until that point when you understand that the ideal must be blended into the real delicately, like the whipped egg whites you use to make a chocolate mousse.

Nathalie. To kiss each other. The fusion of lips and souls. Love. My first novel, written three years earlier at boarding school, elaborated the subject. Nonsense … As if one could know what love was at the age of fifteen! At eighteen I was more sure of myself but knew just as little. I had kissed more girls. That was all.

Just on the other side of the road, a huge façade spangled with windows housed a student residency for young women. Occasionally one would give me the once over and signal to me. I ignored them. I waited for Nathalie. I took on my accursed poet look. I was used to the girls across the way. Some of them wrote me sweet messages. One of them once even scribbled a perfectly blunt message on the entrance door of my apartment building. What a Casanova I was … But not really. I was a romantic, an idealist, an idiot if you will. And I waited for Nathalie.

Who was not showing up.

I would sometimes get up and try to fool my anxiousness by performing perfectly useless tasks (moving a saucepan, or a book; checking how clean the bathroom was), checking the time, then going back to the window to smoke.

Snack time. We were still within the acceptable time slot. She had said around four o'clock. Had she said around four o'clock? If so, she was very late. But Erwan, you know how shopping goes. Sorry. However can I make it up to you? (I had one or two ideas …)

I waited, on the verge of fever and anxiety. Every silhouette that appeared at one of the ends of the street recalled Nathalie for me. Each sound of a motor made my head turn. And what if she had had an accident between Cabriès and Aix? Every time I put out a cigarette, I would take a piece of chewing gum. Just in case we kissed as soon as the door opened. My hands in her long hair … She didn't smoke.

I wouldn't mind eating a pastry, but if she were to arrive and I had crumbs between my teeth … Or worse, greasy fingers.

So, I waited. Now I was angry. Why would she tell me that she was coming for a snack if she wasn't going to come? Nobody forced her, right? I hated her. I wrote sentences about this betrayal. Sentences that would become a poem once they were worked on. A poem about her lie. About her blindness.

Explanation (Nathalie IV)

Liquid Nathalie makes equations about her passions,
An impressive hobby. Imprecise but so close
To the fickle features of the wake of the break-up,
Become undesirable afterward with incursive pretexts.
Untrustworthy, avoided, and praised by default
She takes on false airs, unpredictable passageways,
Of naive innocence, and, false, she displays
An affection void of ruffled reflections;
Suffice it to say that, betrayed, I cast her off.
Hated and homely, Nathalie lies on the ground
Pathetically.
Crushing anger;
Passing.

A snack. Hot chocolate. Sure, right! Nathalie was not there. Nathalie would not be coming. I could feel it but refused to believe it. She said she would stop by for a snack after doing some shopping in town she said so I did not invent that she said that she would stop by with her long brown hair her big almond-shaped eyes her incredible smile she SAID so.

Night was falling. Nathalie and I were made for each other. That was obvious. She knew so, right? Was she scared? And yet it was so simple. Hot chocolate. A kiss. Everything was ready for the snack. For the kiss. For love. Come, Nathalie. I beg you. Come. I called her telepathically. Snack time saw dinner time in its rearview mirror. Nathalie did not exist. Nathalie was a fantasy. Idealized Nathalie that I would not kiss. Nathalie oblivious of my despair, of the madness that was taking me over, of the fangs drilling through my body, of the laughing eyes of the little bitches across the way. I had smoked so much that I didn't have any more chewing gum. Nathalie was alive somewhere but dead to our love. She would not be coming. I wanted a beer, and not this ridiculous hot chocolate, not that tea for overgrown adolescents.

The love I felt for her was tearing me apart. A one-way street. A dead end. Without Nathalie. Never again. I had to stop thinking about her. Over. I wrote words and sentences. I would write a break-up letter. I am leaving you, Nathalie. I am leaving you behind me. Snack time had been over for quite a while now. The shops were closed. She would not be coming. So long, Nathalie. I couldn't trust you. You lied to me. You made a fool of me. It was over.

I wrote many versions of the break-up letter. Built the base for a break-up poem. Farewell, Nathalie. I hated you. I was suffocating. I wanted to talk to someone. I needed to talk to someone. To know if what I was feeling was normal. The suffocation. That laceration, there, inside. To want to die. Anyway, not really, but to have the feeling you wanted to die. Non-sense. Absurd. I needed answers.

She had said that she was going to drop by and see me. She did not come. She would not come. I had looked at it every which way, and she was not there. I grabbed the phone book. My head was turning. A huge creature was scurrying about in my chest. Roaring. Grumbling. It's over, Nathalie. I'm leaving you. That was the day of our first kiss. I had bought tarts and eclairs. You did not come. Bruno Etienne was in the phone book. My professor of political sociology. The man whose course was changing my life.

"The Sykes-Picot Accords. The secret accords of 1916. Do you know them? No, of course not. You bunch of dummies don't know anything. You inanely listen to the talking heads on the evening news!" Professor Bruno Etienne, standing on his desk, after a couple of karate kicks, was a marvel to my seventeen-year-old self. I was finally going to understand the world. Having fewer paths to explore. Doubting. Questioning. A course on the History of Religions in the Politics and Society concentration of the Institute for Political Science. In the Economy and Finance concentration, they didn't have that course. They were preparing for the National School of Administrators, already in a suit and tie. They didn't know anything about the Sykes-Picot Accords that still make blood flow in the East and West one hundred years after they were signed. They would give my cowboy boots a pitying look. Bruno Etienne gave me a hug at the end-of-the-school-year gala after our performance of Pinter's *The Birthday*. He introduced me to Debord and

Bourdieu, Bachelard and Max Weber. He had to know. And he was in the phone book. On which I noticed a scarlet stain. I raised my eyes to the ceiling. Lowered them again. Another stain. I brought my hand to my nose. I was bleeding. For the first time in my life, my nose was bleeding. I think that I called Bruno Etienne, but that no one picked up. I don't know anymore. My nose was bleeding. Because of Nathalie, of her blindness, of her fear, of her selfishness. She had ruined it all. Our beautiful love affair that was only waiting for a snack and a kiss. I would never be in love again. That was decided. There was the evidence. That blood dripping from my nose, so red, so incredibly red, tragically beautiful red, was a sign. It was out of the question to suffer like that because of a woman.

I was eighteen years old. Nathalie did not come. I would never be in love again.

I told this story to Loulou at Castellet, the second stop on the Nocturnes Littéraires book tour. We had met the night before in Saint-Tropez. Sitting next to each other at the bookstore booth, we met, even if nothing appalled me more than a model who had got the idea in her head to write a novel. I am quite a snob when it comes to literature.

The crowd was thin in that little village in the Var countryside, come to meet the authors there. So we decided to leave our seats to go buy olives and rosé wine. We then had an aperitif, chatting behind Loulou's pile of books. "Never be in love again?" She shot back a doubtful pout. No. I had seen friends suffer in the relentless quest for passion. And then destroy themselves by stubbornly loving men who ate away at their self-esteem. Then start all over again, stubborn and ready to get their souls bruised, and sometimes their bodies, for a few magical moments. I had melded passion and tragedy. With love that tears you apart and then eats you up. I would never be in love again. Loulou ate an olive. She found that sad. I made my case even worse with random comparisons. Passionate love was like a raging waterfall in which you almost drown, hard to keep your head above water in the current, tossed about by the waves, as opposed to the lake where feelings surf. If I had wanted to seduce her, I could not have done any worse.

"That's lame," Manuel spurted with a disgusted pout.

"Very lame," Alice sighed.

"Soon you're going to tell us that you have gone over the story line together a hundred times. That you have hunted down the details, the moments. Tried to put words on what magnetically drew you together. And that everything is in harmony. Everything coincides. Everything fits together."

"Oh yeah!" laughed Alice. "You would have to be magnetized! To have *proof!*"

"Irrefutable proof," Manuel guffawed. "You like that adjective, right? You put it in at least two of your earlier novels."

Yes, exactly, my friends! And I was truly very surprised, even flabbergasted, with the realization (you might say that I was the last of the human species to be surprised) that all the laughable, ridiculous situations, grotesque and pathetic, smarmy and silly that I had read about, seen or heard about love, and which I had always gloated over, that all of that hilarious behavior, those ludicrous gestures, those dopey words, had all been inspired by actual facts.

"Oh my! You're lathered up in a soap opera, buddy. Your novel loses all its strength with this sentimental story."

"It's not a sentimental story!" I vehemently protested. "I have fallen in love. But really in love! For the first time."

I understood that the Bataclan had opened a latch, the latch of the blood-stained phone book and Nathalie standing me up. After that episode, I had clipped my emotions. To not risk a brutal blow. I had loved sparingly for years. Which did not exclude the sincerity of my feelings, but limited their breadth.

"Holy cow! Your exes are going to be happy to read that!"

"No, Alice, can't you let up a little? I'll never manage to finish this story if you keep interrupting me!"

"It's a little bit thanks to us that you wrote it, I'd remind you," Manuel interjected. "So we've got the right to say something."

"Above all else because this isn't right at all," Alice bemoaned, shaking her head. "Jeanne was present throughout the whole book. We got attached to her. We suffered with her, and then, Snap! She just melts away."

"I am aware of that. But what to do?"

"Work it out, buddy. It's your manuscript. We're just giving you our opinion."

Thanks, Manuel. That helped a lot.

"Hadn't you talked about a work of literature?"

A work of literature. Yes. But the exercise had then shown its limits. The real balked. The author had nothing to do with it. One of the principal characters had disappeared from the story. The reader would like to know, would like to understand why. Where there any foreboding signs? Between November 13 and August 7, had our hero felt his feelings fritter away? Had he experienced a progressive moment of awareness? Brutal? What were the symptoms? With a true character in a novel, the author, *deus ex machina*, would have had the choice—to explain, to delve into psychology, to scatter clues. But Jeanne exists. And no work of literature can justifiably risk hurting a living person. You won't know anything about it. You will have to imagine it starting out from this injustice—happy endings are not for everybody. And if the end of this chapter does not suit Manuel or Alice, that's not a major problem.

As Seen from Outside: XIV

Mika and I were going to get your motorbike, which
had stayed at the Bataclan. We took my bike, the
glittery one that looked like a party. Yours was black
and old. I don't know why, but I have always imagined
it with bits of duct tape here and there. But to hold
what together? I hopped on the back of my bike, on a
little cushion stuck to the mudguard with suction cups.
There were no foot rests, so my shoe was melting
on the exhaust pipe. Only the right one. Because my
left foot was resting on the sack. Mika drives well.
He's the best driver I know. I held onto him tight.
That was only natural. Because I loved him. We got
to Bastille and headed up Boulevard Richard-Lenoir.
On the other side of the strip, I glimpsed the Saint-
Anne Popincourt Passage, which runs at an angle and
gives onto Rue Nicolas-Appert. I didn't feel well. Two
days before November 13, I was there. With Catherine
and Hélène. Catherine had noticed that on one of
the street signs, Honoré, was missing. Someone had
made four graffiti stencils, with Cabu, Charb, Tignous,
and Wolinski. But no Honoré. So Catherine called
Hélène, Honoré's daughter, and threw out the idea of
making her first street art stencil and, what was most
beautiful, a stencil portrait of the great cartoonist. On
the night of November 11, all three of us decorated
a wall. Honoré had introduced me to Hélène one

May Day for the launch of Melenchon's movement. I was walking alone in the march, and I saw Honoré on the sidewalk. He was so tall. Next to him stood a discreet young woman. That was Hélène. I knew what Kalashnikov bullets could do. The night of November 13, I was in front of my TV. I was watching some kind of bullshit and told myself, "Well, if an attack takes place tonight, I would remember what I was watching." I have forgotten everything. Well, not everything. Mika came back from the garage. He was happy that I was not watching the news. Why? There was an explosion at the Stade de France, and shootings on terraces. I changed channels: the Bataclan. Somebody was at the Bataclan. Who? You. I couldn't breathe anymore. I got up, I sat back down, I opened my mouth like a fish that was going to die. Mika reassured me. "He's not dead. He can't be dead." Why would they kill my friends and leave me alive? "Calm down." Mika was pale. He was scared. Maybe he didn't believe in what he was saying. You wore cowboy boots. A boy who wears cowboy boots would certainly be on the dance floor. Always at the bar. I knew what Kalashnikov bullets could do. At two in the morning, I learned that Richard was dead. I was not aware that he was at the Bataclan. On January 11, with his friends, he posed for a photo holding a sign: "I am Charlie. I am Sigo." I wondered if everything that had happened since January 7 was my fault. Where were you? Answer. Jeanne said, "He left his cell phone at home." Only the emergency number remained. We were still rolling down the street. I held Mika tighter. I was crying under my helmet. Have you ever cried in a helmet? All alone like a stupid fucker, cut off from others by a visor, outside of this world and its happenings. We got to the place where Ahmed Merabet had been killed. There were still flowers there. I didn't feel well. And then there was the Bataclan. My tears stopped. Because Jeanne was there. She was waiting for us in front of the motorcycle. I didn't want her to feel bad. But she was obviously feeling bad. Your bike was behind the red and white security tape. The ribbon was even knotted around the handlebars and rearview mirrors. Jeanne and Mika went to go talk to the police. (Mika, who read over this text, told me otherwise. According to him, Jeanne went to see the police alone.) Your bike was part of the crime scene. I stayed alone next to it and caressed it. I stroked the gas tank. I wanted to be sure that it had not been hit, and that the gas would not leak out. I had done that for Fabrice on January 7. I had stroked his back and torso. I was sure of myself, and told him, "You've only been hit in the legs." I wanted to reassure him. He wouldn't have it. Having your legs ripped up by a Kalashnikov is not just "You've only been hit in the legs." It was serious. The femoral artery was spewing. And there were other bullets, elsewhere in his body. My caresses could not detect them. You had thought you had been hit by two bullets. You were waiting for the third, to your head. You were all white at the hospital. Later on, you showed me your butt and the scars where the bullet entered and exited. They were purple. Jeanne and Mika came back. We released your bike from its trap. Mika and Jeanne got on it. I grabbed my bike's handlebars. It was funny seeing Jeanne behind Mika on your bike, that was rolling at the speed of a moped. You could have almost said it was out of a Roman holiday. On the night of November 13, I thought that you were dead.

29

To TALK ABOUT ANXIETY, or even apprehension, would be going too far.

Despite it all, I couldn't stop myself from thinking about *it* when we got in front of the Olympia. And then going through the bag control and screening, and heading down the long, wide, sloping corridor that led to the lobby. Loulou was holding my hand tightly, and it felt good.

I ran into Virginie. We kissed each other, moved. We hadn't seen each for over ten years. We had worked together at Universal Music. Then France showed up next to the bar, below. We leaped into each other's arms. A hit of pure friendship.

Ringing. We went into the concert hall. We sat down. A light feeling of oppression. Everything was under control, nevertheless. Loulou's presence was at my side, inside, everywhere. Level of paranoia: zero.

Darkness.

The musicians set themselves up. Keren-Ann arrived and started her first number. I suddenly broke down in tears. Loulou dried them and held me close to her. Those were good tears, almost purifying. The love mixed with my fingers was also so purifying.

After a few minutes, the sobs abated.

And there you have it. I had put my butt back inside a concert hall again.

Valencia, Spain.

Loulou and I were drinking a hot chocolate on the terrace of a little café when she realized she had lost the earrings her mother had given her for her birthday. Distress. We had been walking all day long, so it was impossible to just turn around and take our path in the opposite direction. I nevertheless suggested that we retrace our last steps. You never know. We had been walking a few hundred yards, our eyes glued to the sidewalk. Suddenly, I came to a dead stop. In the store window, sitting in a corner on the floor, was a pair of cowboy boots. Superb dark brown boots. I raised my head. It was a secondhand clothing store that we had passed many times before without having noticed it. We went in. I tried on the boots. They were a little too big, but of a remarkable quality, and hardly ever worn.

"They are really beautiful," Loulou told me softly.

I bought them.

And what if I had been at the Bataclan only to have the privilege of meeting Loulou? Say, Lachesis, what do you think about that?

As Seen from Outside: XV

At the Toulon train station. My suitcase was heavy. I
didn't know anybody, and I was hot. I was wearing my
favorite dress, bought in New York City. It had golden,
embroidered daisies on it. My earbuds were protecting
me. I was listening to "Close to Me." Outside, the
sun was bearing down on a guy with a sign. He was
neither a nice guy nor not a nice guy. He had a sign
with my name on it. I like signs with my name on them.
There were other names. I was going to have to talk.
I wanted a shower. I had one drop of lemon-flavored
bottled water left. I was dragging my suitcase behind
me. The guy with the sign made a joke about its size. I
wanted to explain myself. I had to last one month with
that suitcase. I did not want to go back to Paris. I could
not go back. I didn't have a home in Paris anymore.
I would stay in the South, because that's what I had
promised myself. The reasons that forced me to stay
in the South were not funny.

I didn't say anything. I smiled. I was polite, and I
dragged my suitcase.

Got to the car, to the trunk. An older man hurried to
get the passenger seat. He was not a nice guy. He had
the mouth of a guy who was not nice. The attitude as
well. And the rest always follows. I was trying to carry
my suitcase when two hands came to my assistance.

I liked the rings on their fingers. He wore six of them. And an earring too. He had a gap between his front teeth, and gave me a toothy smile. He lifted my suitcase. He was tall, all in black. I thanked him, and got into the back.

In the car, sitting by the window, I looked at his rings. Not the landscape.

It was my third book fair. I had almost refused to come. A week is a real commitment, and I hate commitments. I wanted to be in the South. I was on the port of Saint-Tropez. I found my seat. As did *Bianca*. He had changed clothes. A checkered pair of shorts and a shirt. I had always found shorts ridiculous on men, but the earring made me change my mind. He sat down to my right.

His name was Erwan. You had surely already guessed that.

Not me.

Nor that his room would be next to mine.

Nor that at the moment when we said good night that night, that *thing* would fall on me.

I had wanted to take Nina to *Le Petit Cambodge* for dinner. My sister reproached me for being obsessional. During her last visit, we had gone to *Le Petit*

Cambodge. And the time before, and the time before that. I would always order the same thing: a mixed bo-bun with a Tsingtao. I am obsessional.

I went to pick up Nina at the Gare de l'Est train station. We headed toward the Saint-Martin Canal. She laughed. So I changed destinations.

We were in a Chinese restaurant the night of November 13. Not at *Le Petit Cambodge*. At that moment, in front of Nina, at 10 pm, your gap teeth did not exist.

You whispered a lot. Sometimes I didn't understand. I pretended to, but I did not understand. Something was happening. That *thing*, you know.

You were with me in Room 311, and you had two scars.

I had always loved scars and their stories.

That was before I heard yours. I took you in my arms. I didn't need to understand what you had to say to me. I knew that I was with you. "We" were coming together.

You let me sleep.

See you tomorrow, We.

That night I couldn't keep my eyes closed. Nina couldn't either. I was at a hotel. There are televisions in hotel rooms. Ours was talking about an attack. At *Le Petit Cambodge*. Nina held my hand. I am obsessional, and I could have taken a bullet. Like you. I didn't know you. So I didn't think about you. You were part of a whole. The café terraces. The images of the bodies. Gunfire. Then the Bataclan. The numbers rose. It was huge, and I thought about the waitress at *Le Petit Cambodge*. The one who smiled, with the tattoos. I was wondering if she was among that number. I wasn't thinking about you. I didn't know you.

My grandmother called. The telephone trembled. We reassured her. We were safe. Not you. But I didn't know that. I couldn't imagine it. Léo, my best friend, introduced the group to me. I didn't like their music. I imagined Léo at the Bataclan, and tears welled up in my eyes. I couldn't imagine you there. I didn't know you. Léo was in London, and Nina was sleeping next to me. I ended up going to sleep too.

I don't believe in fate. And yet …

I could have chosen to correct my book in Metz, and not in the South.

Not take a suitcase, just a backpack.

Put on coveralls, because they are comfortable.

Be on the third floor.

You could have forgotten your rings.

Got into another car.

Been seated next to somebody else.

Maintained your literature snob bias. *"A model who writes?"*

You could have missed out on the concert.

You could have died.

You, alive. Room 312.

Me, Room 311.

I didn't want to write. I didn't want to write about you. About you and me. About this story. About those scars that are not part of me.

You wrote that we met each other thanks to them.

I don't agree. I was looking at your rings. I did not know about your scars. I almost didn't meet you. I did meet you, and I loved your gap teeth. The scars came later.

I still don't want to, and yet, I am writing ... my love.

ABOUT THE AUTHOR

ERWAN LARHER was born in central France and attended the prestigious Sciences Po university. He left the music business after 15 years to write full-time; his first novel was published in 2010, and his third, *The Male Abandoned in a Hostile Environment* (2013), won the Claude-Chabrol and the Louis-Barthou literary awards. Larher was shot in the November 13, 2015 attack on the Bataclan Theater, and was lucky to escape with his life; he finished his fourth novel, *Marguerite Doesn't Like Her Butt*, while recovering in hospital. His deeply moving account of this event, *The Book I Didn't Want to Write*, appeared in France in August 2017 and was an immediate critical and commercial success.

Author photo by Emma Picq